MW01122281

2009 03 02

# THE GOLDEN THUG

# THE GOLDEN THUG

## ED ROY

**PLAYWRIGHTS CANADA PRESS**

**TORONTO • CANADA**

**Playwrights Canada Press**
*The Canadian Drama Publisher*
215 Spadina Avenue, Suite 230, Toronto, Ontario CANADA M5T 2C7
416-703-0013 fax 416-408-3402
orders@playwrightscanada.com • www.playwrightscanada.com

This book would be twice its cover price were it not for the support of Canadian taxpayers
through the Government of Canada Book Publishing Industry Development Programme,
the Canada Council for the Arts, the Ontario Arts Council, and the Ontario Media
Development Corporation.

Front cover photo of Andrew Hachey by David Hawe, www.davidhawe.com.
Production Editor: Micheline Courtemanche & JLArt

**Library and Archives Canada Cataloguing in Publication**

Roy, Ed
    The golden thug / Ed Roy.

ISBN 978-0-88754-795-9

1. Genet, Jean, 1910-1986--Drama. I. Title.

PS8585.O89824G64 2008        C812'.54        C2008-901848-6

First edition: April 2008
Printed and bound by Canadian Printco at Scarborough, Canada.

THIS PLAY IS DEDICATED TO THE MEMORY OF

**PAUL BETTIS**

## PLAYWRIGHT'S NOTES

Genet was extremely aware of the power of myth and so he created his own personal mythology. He sprinkled his "biographical novels," plays, magazine articles, and interviews with truths, half-truths, and bald-faced lies. While writing this play and attempting to capture the essence of Genet, I decided to take a cue from the convict poet and delved into his world of self-created myth. So Genet fans be warned, I have sprinkled this play with truths, half-truths and bald-faced lies.

# ACKNOWLEDGEMENTS

Jim LeFrançois, David Oiye, Buddies in Bad Times Theatre, The Theatre Centre, Hume Baugh, Paul Bettis, Shirley Douglas, Allegra Fulton, John Gilbert, Tim Huston, Tanya Jacobs, Moynan King, Maureen Labonté, Andrea Lundy, Sean McComb, Shane Mackinnon, Kristopher Turner, Ty Woolner, David Wooton, Diana Belshaw, Eric Peterson, Christopher Morris, Charles Northcote, Alex Brown, Joyce Goldman, Topological Board of Directors. Extra special thanks: Jacoba Knappen.

*The Golden Thug* was first produced by Topological Theatre in association with Buddies in Bad Times Theatre, in April 2006 with the following company:

| | |
|---|---|
| PIERRE Dargenet | Andrew Hachey |
| GASTON Dargenet | Ralph Small |
| MARIANNE Dargenet | Maria Vacratsis |
| LUC Roland | Dan Watson |
| JEAN Genet | William Webster |

| | |
|---|---|
| Set Design | Charlotte Dean |
| Lighting Design | Bonnie Beecher |
| Costume Design | Angela Thomas |
| Wigs | Alice Norton |
| Sound Design | Kevin O'Leary |
| Production Photos | David Hawe |
| Dramaturge | Maureen Labonté |
| Assistant Director | Keith Fernandes |
| Stage Manager | Amber Archbell |
| Production Manager | Charissa Wilcox |
| Producer | Jim LeFrançois |

# CHARACTERS

JEAN Genet, seventy-six years old
PIERRE Dargenet, seventeen to nineteen years old
MARIANNE Dargenet, late forties to early fifties
GASTON Dargenet, early to mid forties
LUC Roland, twenty years old

# TIME AND PLACE

Paris, April 1986. Jack's Hotel.

*The Golden Thug* is set in a small room in Jack's Hotel, a dingy one-star establishment in the heart of Paris. The furnishings in the room are a mismatched grouping of a single bed, desk, telephone, two chairs, small dresser and a large armoire. There is a large window upstage centre with a recessed windowsill that is framed with tall French Provincial shutters. A tiny lamp sits on the corner of the desk. On one of the walls hangs an ornate crucifix. A light fixture dangles from an electrical cord overhead.

# ACT ONE

## SCENE ONE

*Early morning. MARIANNE Dargenet enters and surveys the room. She crosses over to the bed and fluffs the pillows. GENET enters wearing a well-worn all-weather jacket and scarf. He catches his breath.*

**MARIANNE**

Well here we are, Monsieur. I hope this room is to your liking.

**GENET**

How's the bed?

**MARIANNE**

See for yourself.

> *GENET checks the bed's firmness by lying down on it.*

**GENET**

It'll do. *(He looks up at the ceiling.)* There's a nasty crack in the ceiling.

**MARIANNE**

Yes, I'm afraid this old hotel has seen better days.

**GENET**

Haven't we all?

> *MARIANNE crosses to the door and calls offstage.*

**MARIANNE**

Pierre, what's taking you so long? Pierre! I'm sorry Monsieur, but he must be the laziest kid in Paris for pity's sake!

**GENET**

Laziness is the privilege of youth.

**MARIANNE**

Maybe for the rich, Monsieur, but not mine.

> *GENET exits into the toilet to investigate the amenities as PIERRE Dargenet enters carrying GENET's suitcase. PIERRE is dressed in post-punk '80s clothes and spiked hair. He also wears earphones as his Walkman blasts the song "Master and Servant" by Depeche Mode.*

Ah, here he is, I'm embarrassed to say, dressed like I don't know what. I told you I don't want you dressing like that when you're working.

**PIERRE**
Hein?

**MARIANNE**
I said you're not supposed to dress like that when you're working. *(PIERRE shrugs quizzically.)* I said – oh for God's sake take those stupid things off your ears. *(She pulls one of the earphones out of PIERRE's ear.)* You're going to go deaf playing that thing so loud.

**PIERRE**
Great, then I won't go crazy listening to your nagging.

**MARIANNE**
Hey you watch your mouth, remember who you're talking to. And I don't want you listening to that – that – thing / whatever it's called, while you're working—

**PIERRE**
/ It's called a Walkman—

**MARIANNE**
What I'd like to know is where you got the money to pay for it?

**PIERRE**
I saved up for it. And it wasn't easy with the lousy money you pay me.

**MARIANNE**
Oh quit your complaining. You're lucky I pay you anything at all.

**PIERRE**
I swear if I don't get a raise soon I'll go on strike.

**MARIANNE**
We'll see what your father has to say about that.

> *The sound of the toilet flushing is heard offstage.*

**GENET**
Ah, the toilet works, bravo!

> *GENET re-enters from the toilet.*

**MARIANNE**
Ah, there you are, Monsieur. Where would you like him to put your bag?

**GENET**

At the end of the bed, thank you. *(The light in the room flickers.)*
Is there something wrong with the light? *(The light flickers again.)*
That's going to be very annoying if it keeps on doing that.

**MARIANNE**

Where's your father?

**PIERRE**

I don't know.

**MARIANNE**

What do you know? *(She crosses to the door and calls out.)* Gaston?
Gaston!

**GASTON**

*(offstage)* Yeah, what is it?

**MARIANNE**

I want you to check the light in room seven.

**GASTON**

*(offstage)* What's wrong with it?

**MARIANNE**

How should I know? That's what I keep you around for!

**GASTON**

*(offstage)* All right, all right I'm coming! *(He leans through the doorway and looks up at the light.)* What are you talking about?
It's working just fine.

**MARIANNE**

It was flickering just a moment ago.

**GASTON**

I'll take a look at it after I finish fixing the toilet for the foreigner in room three.

**MARIANNE**

Didn't you just fix it a couple of days ago?

**GASTON**

Marianne, most of the pipes in this place haven't been changed since the Second World War for God's sake!

**MARIANNE**

Oh leave him out of it—

**GENET**

How are the pipes in the one I've got?

**GASTON**

Well if you want to know the truth—

**MARIANNE**

*(She edges GASTON out the door.)* They're just fine, Monsieur. Um, would you just excuse us for a moment?

> *MARIANNE and GASTON exit.*

What's the matter with you? Are you trying to scare away our customers?

> *As MARIANNE and GASTON exit, PIERRE lifts his shirt and wipes away some sweat from his brow. GENET watches him. He stares, mesmerized by PIERRE's casual gesture.*

**GENET**

A bead of sweat snakes down an angel's face like liquid diamonds. A sparkling tributary that frames the youth's divine perfection. It's difficult not to envy this glorious stream that caresses the skin of one so beautiful. I stand humbled... envying the intimacy of sweat.

**PIERRE**

Sweat?

> *GENET begins to gasp for air.*

**GENET**

Oh... I feel dizzy...

**PIERRE**

Monsieur?

**GENET**

Oh...

> *GENET falls back down on the bed. The sound of a cow mooing loudly is heard. GENET and PIERRE are illuminated in an "outhouse" lighting special. MARIANNE enters playing the part of EUGENIE.*

**MARIANNE/EUGENIE**

Jean, you come out of there. You hear me, Jean? You do as you're told and come out of that shithouse!

**GENET**

/ Eugenie?

**PIERRE**

/ Mama.

> *GENET sits up and he and PIERRE look at each other for a moment.*

**MARIANNE/EUGENIE**

Jean, you come out of that shithouse right now or I'll take a switch to you when you do.

**GENET**

I don't care.

**PIERRE**

I'm not coming out.

> *GENET and PIERRE share a smile of recognition.*

**MARIANNE/EUGENIE**

Where did you get those candies, hein? *(beat)* How do you think it makes me feel when people tell me I'm raising a little thief in my house? I won't have it! This village is too small to get a reputation for stealing. Now tell me, where did you get those candies?

**GENET**

I bought them.

**MARIANNE/EUGENIE**

Oh really? And where did you get the money?

**PIERRE**

I made it singing with the choir at Monsieur Barbezat's funeral after school today.

**MARIANNE/EUGENIE**

I thought you weren't going to sing at funerals anymore because Abbé Charrault still owed you boys money from the last three?

**GENET**

Well, he finally paid up.

> *Suddenly GASTON enters in the role of ABBÉ Charrault. PIERRE assumes the role of YOUNG GENET.*

**GASTON/ABBÉ**

Jean, how dare you lead a strike against the church? My church!

**PIERRE/YOUNG GENET**

Monsieur Abbé, if you want us chickadees to warble at Monsieur Barbezat's funeral today I suggest you pay your debts.

**GASTON/ABBÉ**

Pay my debts indeed! It's unchristian to strike against the church!

**PIERRE/YOUNG GENET**

As I recall our Lord started out in life as a carpenter but I don't remember reading anything about him giving his cabinets away for free.

**GASTON/ABBÉ**

But think of poor Madame Barbezat. How am I going to tell her that there will be no singing at her husband's funeral? I would have thought a person, such as yourself, who has lived on the charity of the state since the day he was born would have a little more compassion for others in their hour of need.

**PIERRE/YOUNG GENET**

Even orphans are capable of feeling compassion, Monsieur Abbé. So why don't I just go and explain the situation to Madame Barbezat?

**GASTON/ABBÉ**

You'll do no such thing! Here.

> *The ABBÉ produces a bag of coins. He hands it to PIERRE/YOUNG GENET.*

It's all that's owed plus today.

> *PIERRE/YOUNG GENET examines the contents of the bag.*

Now put your robe back on and tell the choir the strike is over. And for God's sake don't dawdle, *(as he exits)* it's boiling out there today and Madame Barbezat is wearing a dress that's two sizes too small for her!

**MARIANNE/EUGENIE**

He just gave you the money?

**GENET**

Maybe he was suffering from a guilty conscience.

> *PIERRE/YOUNG GENET and GENET snicker and giggle.*

**MARIANNE/EUGENIE**

You bought a lot of candy.

**PIERRE/YOUNG GENET**

We sang particularly well today.

**MARIANNE/EUGENIE**

Then why didn't you say so? Why do you make things so difficult, hein?

**PIERRE/YOUNG GENET**

Today in school our teacher gave us our marks for a paper we were assigned to write describing each of our houses.

**GENET**

The teacher said mine was the best written and then he read it to the class.

**MARIANNE/EUGENIE**

Isn't that wonderful?

**PIERRE/YOUNG GENET**

All the other kids laughed and made fun of me. They said it wasn't really my house because I'm a "foster child."

**MARIANNE/EUGENIE**

They were just jealous because you wrote the best paper.

*GENET lies down on the bed.*

**GENET**

It was humiliating. They made me feel like a foreigner.

**MARIANNE/EUGENIE**

That's nonsense, you were born in France just like the rest of them.

**PIERRE/YOUNG GENET**

But didn't you know, Mama? You're not really a citizen of France if you lack the proper pedigree.

**MARIANNE/EUGENIE**

Stop talking foolishness. It'll be time for supper soon and I'll be expecting you at the table or you'll go without. And maybe if I make a special dessert you'll read your paper to us? Mmm? Now you come out of that shithouse before somebody has to use it for something other than sulking.

*MARIANNE/EUGENIE exits as the lighting in the room returns to the present.*

**PIERRE**

Monsieur, Monsieur what's wrong? Monsieur? *(He runs to the door.)* Mama! Mama come quick!

**MARIANNE**

*(offstage)* What is it now?

**PIERRE**

It's the old guy in room seven, there's something wrong with him—

**MARIANNE**

*(offstage)* I'm coming, I'm coming!

**PIERRE**

Monsieur do you want some water? Should I get water?

> PIERRE *exits into the bathroom as* MARIANNE *and* GASTON *enter.*

**MARIANNE**

Oh no – Monsieur? What happened?

> MARIANNE *begins to check for* GENET'*s vital signs.* PIERRE *re-enters from the bathroom with a glass of water.*

**PIERRE**

I don't know. He just started gasping for air, then he fainted.

**GASTON**

Maybe he's having a stroke or something.

**MARIANNE**

Monsieur, Monsieur can you hear me?

> GENET *begins to stir.*

**GENET**

Eugenie?

**MARIANNE**

No, Monsieur, it's me, Madame Dargenet.

**GENET**

Oh yes…

**MARIANNE**

Should I call an ambulance?

**GENET**

Mmm? No…. I'm all right…. I just blacked out for a moment…. It's just so stuffy in here… could someone open the window?

**MARIANNE**

Gaston, open the window.

> GASTON *tries to open the window as* PIERRE *passes the glass of water to* MARIANNE.

Here, take a sip of this.

**GENET**

Thank you.

**GASTON**

The window's stuck, it won't budge.

**MARIANNE**

Well that's one more thing for you to fix. How are you feeling, Monsieur?

**GENET**

Better… must have been the heat…. I didn't get any sleep on the train, and those front stairs.

**MARIANNE**

You're sure you're all right?

**GENET**

Yes.

> *The light flickers.*

**MARIANNE**

You see?

**GASTON**

Yeah, okay, I'll get to it.

**GENET**

I don't want to spend my time trying to work with that thing going on and off.

**MARIANNE**

If you don't mind me asking, what kind of work will you be doing, Monsieur?

**GENET**
> I'm a writer.

**GASTON**
> Haven't had a writer stay with us for a while.

**MARIANNE**
> You know he kind of reminds me of Monsieur Grasset. Remember he was the gentleman who stayed in room nineteen two years ago? He was also a writer. Remember him?

**GASTON**
> Yeah you're right, he does kind of look like him.

**MARIANNE**
> His writing could really tug at your heart and then flip on a dime and bring a smile to your face. He could write to fit any occasion.

**GENET**
> Oh really, what kind of writing did he do?

**MARIANNE**
> Greeting cards.

**GENET**
> Greeting cards?

**MARIANNE**
> He was very talented.

**GASTON**
> Made a decent living too.

**MARIANNE**
> I sent one of his own condolence cards to his family when I heard he passed away.

**GENET**
> How touching.

**PIERRE**
> Have you written anything I might have heard of?

**GENET**
> I don't think so.

**MARIANNE**
> Enough talk, I'm sorry, Monsieur, but he's got more work to do.

**PIERRE**

But—

**GASTON**

No buts, do as you're told.

**PIERRE**

All right, all right, I'm going.

*PIERRE starts to put the Walkman earphones back on.*

**MARIANNE**

What did I say about listening to that while you're working?

*PIERRE turns the Walkman volume up loud and exits.*

**GENET**

What about the light?

**GASTON**

I'll take care of it as soon as I clean up the flood in room three. Shouldn't be more than a couple of hours if that's okay?

**MARIANNE**

As long as you come back and fix it before the end of the day.

**GASTON**

I said I'd be back in a couple of hours / didn't I?

**MARIANNE**

/ You say a lot of things but that doesn't necessarily mean / you're going to do them.

**GASTON**

/ Nothing's going to get done standing here arguing with you.

*GASTON exits as MARIANNE calls out to him.*

**MARIANNE**

And don't forget to fix this window. I hope you enjoy your stay with us, Monsieur, and if you need anything else just call me at the front desk.

**GENET**

Thank you, Madame.

*MARIANNE exits.*

*As GENET crosses to his suitcase he suffers from a sudden spasm of pain in his throat. Inhaling deeply, he maintains control as he opens the suitcase. He removes a bottle of pills from it and waits for a moment hoping the pain will subside. After a few beats GENET regains control and puts the unopened bottle of pills back in his suitcase. He takes out a leopard skin patterned notebook and begins writing.*

*Blackout.*

## SCENE TWO

*Late afternoon. The same day. Lights come up on GENET sitting at the desk writing in the leopard notebook. The contents of GENET's suitcase have begun to spill into the room. A few notebooks with different cover designs lie open on the bed. There is a stack of fresh white paper on the desk along with other writing paraphernalia. There is the sound of someone knocking on the door.*

**GENET**
Huh? Yes? Who is it?

**PIERRE**
*(offstage)* A package has arrived for you, Monsieur.

> *GENET continues to write without looking up from his notebook.*

**GENET**
Oh yes um… come in, the door's open.

> *PIERRE enters holding a large brown envelope.*

You said something arrived?

**PIERRE**
*(holds up the envelope)* Yeah.

> *GENET puts the notebook down and turns to PIERRE.*

**GENET**
Oh, my dear, I've been waiting for you.

**PIERRE**
Pardon?

> *GENET snatches the package from PIERRE's hands.*

**GENET**

I've had many lovers in my life, Pierre, but not one has ever compared to this.

**PIERRE**

What is it?

> *GENET rips open the envelope and removes his manuscript.*

**GENET**

My words.

**PIERRE**

Words?

**GENET**

Sometimes they shoot from me like streams of ejaculate.

**PIERRE**

Pardon?

**GENET**

Um?

**PIERRE**

Uh…. It's just that… you said words shoot out of you – like streams of…?

**GENET**

Like streams of cum. Yes. They do.

**PIERRE**

I don't get you.

**GENET**

You know what it's like when you're alone and absolutely certain no one will disturb you? Alone enough to stare into a mirror naked and truly give yourself over to that imaginary lover in your mind? Alone enough to ravage yourself? Know what that's like?

**PIERRE**

Uh huh…

**GENET**

And when you can no longer endure the self-torture of "delayed gratification" – when you're finally ready to…

**PIERRE**

Cum?

**GENET**

Yes. And cum and cum and—

**PIERRE**

Cum until you almost hurt yourself?

**GENET**

Yes! Sometimes that's how it feels when the words come.

**PIERRE**

You're a dirty old man.

**GENET**

Age has nothing to do with it. Words have always made me horny.

**PIERRE**

*(He laughs.)* So what's this thing that's making you so horny called?

**GENET**

*Prisoner of Love.*

**PIERRE**

Good title.

**GENET**

Glad you like it.

**PIERRE**

What's it about?

**GENET**

A man named Yasser Arafat asked me to write a book about the plight of his people. He wants the world to know about their struggle and suffering. He thought I could help.

**PIERRE**

Why you?

**GENET**

Because I'm for the underdog. The thief, whore, faggot, maggot! I am the Black American who wants equality, the Palestinian who wants his land back – the underdog incarnate who will always gnaw at the heels of my universal oppressor.

**PIERRE**

You hate Jews?

**GENET**

My dear boy, if the Jews were ejected from Israel today I would be championing their cause tomorrow.

**PIERRE**

That's just fucked. How can you think that way?

**GENET**

I'm French, it's in our genes. *(beat)* And soon I'll be finished my final draft and then…. It's in Gallimard's hands.

**PIERRE**

Gallimard?

**GENET**

My publisher. But that won't happen unless I get back to work, so if you'll excuse me.

*GENET begins to look over his manuscript.*

**PIERRE**

Uh, Monsieur?

*GENET continues to focus on the manuscript.*

What did you mean when you said you envied the intimacy of sweat?

**GENET**

Um?

**PIERRE**

That's what you said just before you fainted. You said something about liquid diamonds and envying the intimacy of sweat.

**GENET**

Did I? Mmm…. Liquid diamonds? Liquid diamonds…. Liquid – A sparkling tributary…. Yes – yes— *(He picks up the notebook and begins writing in it.)* I remember – yes – A bead of sweat snakes down an angel's face like liquid diamonds. / A sparkling tributary—

**PIERRE**

/ Yeah, that's it—

**GENET**

That frames the youth's divine perfection, this glorious stream that caresses the skin – I stand humbled...

**PIERRE**

Envying the intimacy of sweat.

**GENET**

It's good isn't it? I hope I can use it somewhere.

*GENET jots down a final note.*

**PIERRE**

So what made you say it?

**GENET**

Oh I don't know um... psychic leakage? Freudian hot flash? Maybe a spark of recognition of qualities I once possessed but have now flown out of memory? Who knows what entices the muse to lift the veil? I'm just grateful when she deigns to bless me with her kiss.

**PIERRE**

So how many books have you written?

**GENET**

Five.

**PIERRE**

Only five?

**GENET**

Some people need to write a hundred books to get their point of view across. I only needed to write five. And then I started writing plays.

**PIERRE**

Oh, you write plays, too?

**GENET**

They've been produced here in Paris, London, Berlin. In fact one of my plays ran for four years in New York City. And a couple of them have been made into movies.... Not very good ones.

**PIERRE**

Yeah right.

**GENET**

Those idiot producers should have let me direct.

**PIERRE**

So how come I've never heard of you?

**GENET**

"For a long time I used to go to bed early." Do you know who wrote those words?

**PIERRE**

No.

**GENET**

Proust, ever heard of him? What about Rimbaud? Zola? Hegel?

**PIERRE**

Are those guys famous writers?

**GENET**

They were but apparently their clout is diminishing by the minute.

**PIERRE**

Do people read your books?

**GENET**

Do people still read?

**PIERRE**

Smartass.

**GENET**

*Merci*, I'll take that as a compliment.

**PIERRE**

Take it however you like.

**GENET**

I usually like to take it up the ass.

**PIERRE**

So you're queer, uh?

**GENET**

Does that bother you?

**PIERRE**

Not as long as you don't get any funny ideas.

**GENET**

What a curse to lay on a writer.

**PIERRE**

You know what I mean.

**GENET**

*Mon cher* believe me, you could never compete with the erotic charge this gives me. *(clutching his manuscript)* Besides look at me, do I look strong enough to force you to do anything you don't want to do?

**PIERRE**

I guess not.

**GENET**

It was ever thus.

**PIERRE**

What?

**GENET**

Straight guys always feel less threatened around a faggot that's half-dead. No fear of being taken from behind when the beast hasn't got any strength left in its haunches. *(The light flickers.)* I hope your father remembers he's still got to fix that. Maybe you could do me a favour and go and remind him? *(He returns to his manuscript.)*

**PIERRE**

Sure, but it just seems kind of weird that you got your plays produced in those cities and into movies and whatever, and you end up having to stay in a hole like this.

**GENET**

This is a palace compared to some of the holes I've spent time in.

> *PIERRE moves to exit.*

**PIERRE**

I'll bet.

> *GENET looks up from his manuscript.*

**GENET**

Holes that stank with the sweat, shit and piss of hundreds of naked men and boys who screamed at cold stone walls that were deaf to their misery. Walls that witnessed the flaying of loneliness until all that was left of the victims was a pitiless pulp.

**PIERRE**

Are you talking about prison?

**GENET**

Our shame gave us comfort when we were naked. Our farts filled the air with a sweeter fragrance than the flowers that held us captive.

**PIERRE**

You saying you were in prison? Bullshit.

**GENET**

Is it?

**PIERRE**

What did you do?

**GENET**

Wouldn't you like to know?

**PIERRE**

I don't really give a shit.

**GENET**

Of course not, I'm sure you have much better things to do.

*GASTON calls from offstage.*

**GASTON**

*(offstage)* Pierre? Pierre!

**GENET**

Oh wait, isn't that your papa I hear calling you?

**PIERRE**

Fuck you.

**GENET**

Such language.

**PIERRE**

So were you?

**GASTON**

*(offstage)* Pierre?

**GENET**

Ever in prison?

**PIERRE**

Yeah.

**GENET**
Ever kissed a guy?

**PIERRE**
What?

*The sound of footsteps are approaching in the hallway.*

**GASTON**
*(offstage)* Pierre? Where is that kid?

**PIERRE**
Shhhh… *(whispering)* He's relentless, he's probably got another dumb-ass job for me to do. God I can't wait to get out of this place.

*PIERRE leans against the wall next to the door. There is a lighting shift and PIERRE/YOUNG GENET is transported to the "Boys' Prison of Mettray" circa 1923. The silhouette of the actor playing LUC, in the role of VILLEROY, appears "through" the wall that PIERRE is leaning against. LUC/VILLEROY's facial features should remain in the shadows throughout the scene.*

**LUC/VILLEROY**
Jean, what do you think you're doing?

**PIERRE/YOUNG GENET**
I'm getting out of here.

**LUC/VILLEROY**
Are you nuts? Nobody's ever escaped. And then when they catch you, you'll end up in solitary.

**PIERRE/YOUNG GENET**
Either way I'll get a break from milking those bloody cows.

**GENET**
Besides whoever heard of a son of Zeus milking a cow?

**LUC/VILLEROY**
Hein?

**PIERRE/YOUNG GENET**
Didn't you know, Villeroy?

**GENET**
I was born out of the head of Zeus like fair Athena herself.

**LUC/VILLEROY**

I had no idea.

**PIERRE/YOUNG GENET**

Yes, one day I fell off Mount Olympus and landed here, where I'm forced to squeeze cow teats for eternity.

**LUC/VILLEROY**

You'll be shovelling cow shit for eternity as well if they catch you trying to escape.

**PIERRE/YOUNG GENET**

All we have to do is get to the train station. / Then we can hop a train to Nice—

**LUC/VILLEROY**

We?

**PIERRE/YOUNG GENET**

Why not? You hate being stuck in here as much as I do.

**GENET**

Come with me to Egypt.

**LUC/VILLEROY**

Egypt?

**PIERRE/YOUNG GENET**

You want to come see the pyramids?

**LUC/VILLEROY**

We can't go to Egypt. / We'll never make it.

**GENET**

/ Then how about America?

**PIERRE/YOUNG GENET**

Greece?

**GENET**

The world is a banquet waiting to be feasted on.

**LUC/VILLEROY**

Nobody sits at the table for free, Jean. How do you expect us to survive without a trade or any money?

**PIERRE/YOUNG GENET**

By our wits and beauty.

Dan Watson, William Webster and Andrew Hachey
*photo by David Hawe*

**LUC/VILLEROY**
That's how I ended up here in the first place.

**GENET**
So you accept the fate doled out to you?

**LUC/VILLEROY**
Better that than starving in the streets or worse, starving in solitary.

**PIERRE/YOUNG GENET**
That remains to be seen.

**LUC/VILLEROY**
Well for what it's worth, I hope you make it.

**PIERRE/YOUNG GENET**
Thanks.

**LUC/VILLEROY**

I'll miss you if you do. *(beat)* You think you'll miss me?

**GENET**

I shall carry you in a pocket sewn to my heart forever.

*The sound of footsteps approaching.*

**LUC/VILLEROY**

Shhh... someone's coming. Shit, it's Lardet. If you're going to run you better do it now. But remember, if you make it to the flower bushes, don't touch any of the flowers, they're electrified.

*He exits as GASTON/LARDET appears out of the darkness.*

**PIERRE/YOUNG GENET**

Electrified?

**GASTON/LARDET**

*(voice-over)* I've been looking for you number 192.102.

*Beat. Lights fade on GASTON/LARDET and we return to the present.*

**GASTON**

*(offstage)* Pierre! Where has that kid gone off to?

*GASTON moves off down the hall.*

**PIERRE**

Whew, that was close. *(He looks at GENET who is fanning himself with the manuscript.)* Hey, Monsieur, you okay? Don't want you fainting on me again.

**GENET**

I'm – I'm fine.... So, ever kissed a guy?

**PIERRE**

Ever been to prison?

**GENET**

I'll tell you if you tell me. And please no family members unless you've got some juicy tale of incest.

**PIERRE**

Now you're being gross.

**GENET**

Look you've wasted enough of my time hanging around here trying to avoid work, so unless you're going to make it interesting—

**PIERRE**

Yeah, so I kissed a guy, big deal. What about you?

**GENET**

Oh yeah, plenty of times.

**PIERRE**

No, I'm talking about being in prison.

**GENET**

Oh yeah, plenty of times.

**PIERRE**

Like how many?

**GENET**

Oh gee, let's see. Mmmm… about twenty?

**PIERRE**

Twenty?

**GENET**

Give or take a couple.

**PIERRE**

You're shitting me.

**GENET**

Not a fetish I was ever particularly fond of.

**PIERRE**

You're serious?

**GENET**

I spent so much time behind bars the outside world almost lost me.

**PIERRE**

What'd you do?

**GENET**

Just about everything they tell you you'll go to hell for.

**PIERRE**

You ever kill anyone?

**GENET**

Did you like kissing that guy?

**PIERRE**

You're disgusting.

**GENET**

Guilty. So?

**MARIANNE**

(offstage) Pierre?

**PIERRE**

If I told Mama what you were on about she'd kick you out on your ass.

**GENET**

No one's stopping you.

> MARIANNE arrives at GENET's door and knocks.

**MARIANNE**

Excuse me Monsieur, I'm sorry to disturb you but have you seen Pierre? I sent him up here with a package.

**GENET**

Yes, come in, he's here.

**MARIANNE**

(She enters.) What's taking you so long? Your father's been looking for you. He's expecting you to help him take the garbage out to the street.

**GENET**

I wanted to smell the spring air and he was helping me open the window but it's still stuck.

**MARIANNE**

You couldn't get it open?

**PIERRE**

Ah... no.... It'll probably need a crowbar.

**MARIANNE**

I thought I told your father to fix that? I'm sorry, Monsieur; I'll make sure he sees to it.

> The light flickers.

**GENET**

And please don't forget about the light.

**MARIANNE**

Yes, yes of course. Well what are you waiting for? Go help your father before the garbage truck comes.

> *GENET picks up his manuscript.*

**GENET**

Yes, we all have work to do.

**PIERRE**

Okay, okay.

> *PIERRE exits followed by MARIANNE.*

**MARIANNE**

Good afternoon, Monsieur.

> *She exits. GENET puts down his manuscript and picks up the leopard notebook. He chuckles to himself as he begins to write in it.*
>
> *Blackout.*

## SCENE THREE

> *The next day. Mid-afternoon. Lights come up on PIERRE sitting on the window with a crowbar at his side. LUC Roland leans against the window frame. LUC is shirtless and PIERRE is wearing a T-shirt. They share a cigarette. There is more of GENET's writing strewn about the room. The wastepaper basket is full of crumpled pages. However, the desk, where the manuscript is, remains pristine. After a few beats GENET enters with his sleeves rolled up, carrying his jacket.*

**PIERRE**

You're back already?

**GENET**

I thought you'd have it opened by now.

**LUC**

Piece of shit won't budge.

**GENET**

Who's your friend?

**LUC**

(*He extends his hand.*) Luc.

**GENET**

Jean, a pleasure.

**PIERRE**

Luc dropped by to pick me up because we were supposed to hang out but my old lady said I couldn't go until I get this ball-buster open for you.

**LUC**

Haven't your parents ever heard of air conditioning?

**PIERRE**

Oh, they've heard of it. They just don't want to pay for it.

**GENET**

Whatever happened to spring? It's only April and it's already hotter than hell.

**LUC**

I like hot weather.

**GENET**

If I had a body like yours I'd like it, too.

**LUC**

I'll put my T-shirt back on if you like.

**GENET**

No, please, this room needed something pretty to distract from the dreary wallpaper.

**LUC**

I bet you'd like to see a little more.

**GENET**

Not if it's truly little.

       *GENET picks up the leopard notebook and jots down notes.*

**LUC**

Ha, so it's true what Pierre told me about you.

**GENET**

Has Pierre been talking about me? How flattering.

**PIERRE**

Luc we better get this open because she's going to check it before she lets me get / out of here.

**LUC**

/ Pierre said you were some queer writer who went to prison.

**PIERRE**

Luc—

**GENET**

I'd say that encapsulates my life pretty accurately. Maybe that's what I should have put on my gravestone: "Here lies some queer writer that went to prison."

**LUC**

So what's it like?

**GENET**

It's great if you like sucking cock.

**LUC**

I meant prison.

**GENET**

So did I.

**LUC**

You know I went to juvenile detention for a few months just last year.

**GENET**

Really? What did they pin you for?

**LUC**

Shoplifting.

> PIERRE tries to pry the window open.

**GENET**

Your first offence?

**LUC**

Nah.

> PIERRE grunts as he applies pressure to the crowbar.

My parents really flipped out.

**GENET**

You better be careful, it can become addictive.

**LUC**

Shoplifting?

**GENET**

Prison.

*GENET returns his attention to the manuscript.*

**PIERRE**

Ah, you mother, come on.... Shit!

**LUC**

Hey, keep it down over there.

**PIERRE**

Screw you!

**LUC**

Many have tried.

*GENET looks up from the manuscript.*

**GENET**

While you're on that subject; did you manage to hold onto your virginity while you were incarcerated?

**LUC**

It wasn't easy that's for sure, but yes, I managed to, thank you very much.

**GENET**

In my day you would've been lucky to hold on to your cherry for one night tops if you were as pretty as you are. Even if you weren't so pretty. But I was.

**LUC**

Were you ever raped?

*There is a dramatic lighting change and we are transported to the "Boys' Prison of Mettray" circa 1923. The actor playing the role of GASTON enters and he, along with the actor playing LUC, assume the roles of the boy inmates of Mettray; LUC/VILLEROY and GASTON/BOY ONE.*

**LUC/VILLEROY**
Hey, kid, what're you looking for?

**PIERRE/YOUNG GENET**
I'm trying to find my hammock.

**GASTON/BOY ONE**
He's a little lost lamb.

**LUC/VILLEROY**
Why'd they send you here?

**PIERRE/YOUNG GENET**
I – I gouged out the eyes of some cop.

**GENET/BOY TWO**
Ooooo.

**PIERRE/YOUNG GENET**
Didn't know a guy could bleed like a pig through the eyes.

**GASTON/BOY ONE**
He doesn't look that tough to me.

**LUC/VILLEROY**
Hey, squirt, you tough enough to keep the big shots out of your pants?

**GENET/BOY TWO**
Looks like he's about to shit his pants.

**GASTON/BOY ONE**
Hey maybe we ought to plug something up there so he doesn't make a mess. Who's going to corn-hole this little squab first?

**GENET/BOY TWO**
Come over here cutie, my hammock's big enough for two.

**GASTON/BOY ONE**
That's not the only thing you've got that's big enough for two!
*(boys laugh)*

**LUC/VILLEROY**
Screw you guys, that little chicken's mine tonight.

**GASTON/BOY ONE**
What are we arguing about? We can all give him a poke!

**PIERRE/YOUNG GENET**

(*He sings the song, "My Lover's Lips" by Ed Roy.*)
My lover's lips were red like wine.
Her eyes so blue her smile divine. /

**LUC/VILLEROY**

/ Hey, listen to that. He's a regular songbird.

**PIERRE/YOUNG GENET**

(*singing*) Intoxicating love makes men blind.
My lover's lips were red like wine. /

**GASTON/BOY ONE**

/ It's a pretty catchy tune.

**PIERRE/YOUNG GENET**

(*singing*) My lover sleeps beneath the ground.
I held the gun that shot her down.
Together I found them without making a sound.
My lover sleeps beneath the ground.

*When he stops singing there is applause.*

**GENET/BOY TWO**

Come on, cutie, sing us another one.

**GASTON/BOY ONE**

Yeah, sing us another one.

**LUC/VILLEROY**

He's finished his singing for tonight, chumps, now piss off.

**GASTON/BOY ONE**

Come on, fellas, let's go. Looks like Villeroy beat us to it.

*GASTON/BOY ONE retreats to his place by the door and acts as a lookout.*

**LUC/VILLEROY**

Where'd you learn that little ditty?

**GENET**

Paris.

**LUC/VILLEROY**

Know any others?

**PIERRE/YOUNG GENET**
Plenty.

**LUC/VILLEROY**
What's your name?

**GENET**
Jean...

**PIERRE/YOUNG GENET**
Val Jean.

**LUC/VILLEROY**
Where have I heard that name before?

**GENET**
A history book maybe?

**LUC/VILLEROY**
Doubt it.

**PIERRE/YOUNG GENET**
My father's family were descendants of the Plan-tage-Genets.

**LUC/VILLEROY**
Well, Your Highness, I don't think you really have it in you to gouge out the eyes of a cop. So how'd you really end up in here? *(beat)*

**PIERRE/YOUNG GENET**
I ran away because the state was sending me off to school to become a typographer.

**GENET**
Who the fuck wants to become a typographer?

**PIERRE/YOUNG GENET**
Magician, acrobat, master criminal; anything but typographer!

**GENET**
But it was out of my hands.

**PIERRE/YOUNG GENET**
It was decided and I was just supposed to kiss their asses and be grateful for the life of boring mediocrity they were ramming down my throat.

**GENET**
So I ran away...

**PIERRE/YOUNG GENET**
Got caught stealing.

*Beat.*

**LUC/VILLEROY**
You ever been screwed?

**GENET**
Since the day I was born.

**LUC/VILLEROY**
Any of us could say the same. Still, you'll need someone to protect you in here or a different guy will bugger you every night.

**PIERRE/YOUNG GENET**
I could think of worse fates.

**LUC/VILLEROY**
Suit yourself. But some of the guys around here like it pretty rough. *(He moves to exit.)*

**GENET**
No wait…

**PIERRE/YOUNG GENET**
Don't go.

**LUC/VILLEROY**
Hey, don't sweat it. If anybody tries to mess with you just let them know that they'll have to answer to Villeroy. You got that?

**GENET**
Villeroy.

*LUC/VILLEROY gives PIERRE/YOUNG GENET a light kiss on the lips.*

**LUC/VILLEROY**
Now you go and find your hammock and I'll come and see you after lights out.

**PIERRE/YOUNG GENET**
*(He walks back toward the window.)* Sure…

**GENET**
Enough!

*The lighting snaps to the present.*

**LUC**

Hein?

**GENET**

Why would I open my heart to you?

**PIERRE**

Hey, Luc, will you leave him alone?

**LUC**

What? He asked me if I got screwed so I asked him.

*GENET picks up the leopard notebook and writes.*

**GENET**

Yes, yes of course… I asked for it.

**PIERRE**

Just get over here and help me.

**LUC**

/ Will you relax? The fucking thing's stuck, you're going to need a jackhammer to / get it open.

**PIERRE**

/ But Mama won't let me out / if we don't…

**LUC**

/ You sound like a fucking pussy. / "Mama, oh Mama won't let me go out!" / Jesus can't you take a shit yet without asking "Mama's" permission?

**PIERRE**

/ You said you'd help. / We made a deal remember? I'll only lend you the money if you help me get this open.

**GENET**

Hey, I can't concentrate with you two arguing like an old married couple!

*LUC crosses to the window.*

**LUC**

Okay let's give it another go and see if we can make Grandpa here and your mama happy.

**PIERRE**

I think if we try to open it together at the spot I just tried…

**LUC**

We'll both end up with hernias.

> *They try to pry the window open with the crowbar.*

**PIERRE**

/ Urgh…

**LUC**

/ Urgh…

> *The boys continue to work as we are transported back to the "Boys' Prison of Mettray." GASTON/LARDET appears silhouetted in the doorway. During GASTON/LARDET's speech we hear the voice-overs of the boys of Mettray.*

**GASTON/LARDET**

/ Welcome to Mettray, number 192.102.

> *GENET slams the notebook down on the desk. PIERRE stops working and faces GASTON/LARDET while LUC/VILLEROY continues to work.*

**LUC/VILLEROY**

/ Urgh…

**GASTON/LARDET**

/ I am the director of the colony, Monsieur Lardet. On your knees! Prayer!

> *PIERRE/YOUNG GENET remains standing as LUC/VILLEROY drops to his knees and prays along with the boys of Mettray.*

**BOYS OF METTRAY**

*(voice-over)* My God, I thank you for letting me live through another day.

**GASTON/LARDET**

Let it be so! Despite what you might have heard number 192.102, the colony of Mettray is not a prison for boys. We are an agricultural commune of "supervised freedom."

**BOYS OF METTRAY**

*(voice-over)* Please give me the blessing of sleeping well tonight.

**GASTON/LARDET**

Let it be so! In this place the ideals of Rousseau prevail. There are no walls or fences, only laurel bushes and flowerbeds. Fresh air and plenty of sunlight nourish the soil and purify the soul.

**BOYS OF METTRAY**

(voice-over) May you take pity on us and protect our parents, friends and benefactors.

**GASTON/LARDET**

Let it be so! The day begins at five a.m. Toilet, wash, dress, prayer and two hours of work before breakfast. Three more hours of work then lunch. Three more hours of work followed by one hour of study, supper, evening prayer, song, and to bed at nine o'clock.

**BOYS OF METTRAY**

(voice-over) Please grant us the blessings to be worthy of your love. And please let it be over, let it be over, let it be over!

**GASTON/LARDET**

Silence! Sleep! I hope your stay with us will be educational and uneventful 192.102. And that you will leave this place a better person. So once again, welcome to Mettray.

> The lights go to black except for the light coming through the window. GASTON stands silhouetted in the doorway.

**GASTON**

What's going on in here?

**PIERRE**

We were trying to get the window open and the light went out.

**GENET**

You said you'd fix it yesterday!

**GASTON**

I'm sorry, Monsieur, but you know how it is...

**GENET**

Yes, it's damned inconvenient that's what it is! I can't think straight with that damn thing going on and off! I've had to put up with this bullshit for a day and a half! I'm on a tight deadline and I won't stay another night unless you fix it immediately.

**GASTON**

That's why I'm here, Monsieur.

*The light flickers back on.*

**GENET**

Good.

*GENET turns his attention to his manuscript.*

**GASTON**

What's he doing here?

**LUC**

It's nice to see you too, Monsieur Dargenet.

**PIERRE**

He was helping me.

**GASTON**

What's the matter? You bored with high society?

**LUC**

No, I'm just bored with everything in general, and right now in particular, the direction this conversation is taking.

**PIERRE**

Look we tried to get the window open but couldn't so what do you want me to do?

**GASTON**

Say goodbye to your little friend.

**PIERRE**

But…

**GASTON**

Bye-bye, Luc.

**PIERRE**

But Mama said…

**GASTON**

That you could go out when the window was opened. But it isn't so, so-long Luc.

**PIERRE**

/ Oh come on…

**LUC**

*(He picks up his T-shirt and puts it on.)* / No, it's okay, call me when you're done, I'll be at Louis's. Nice meeting you, Jean, and Monsieur

Dargenet... a pleasure as always. Oh uh, Pierre, you mind giving me that money before I head out?

**PIERRE**

But...

**GASTON**

Well, you going to give him his money or not?

> *PIERRE removes a small role of francs from his pocket and gives it to LUC.*

**LUC**

Thanks. See you later.

> *LUC exits. The light flickers again and remains on.*

**GASTON**

Yeah, could be the fuse or a faulty connection somewhere. The wiring in this place is so old, the insulation is just rotting off.

**GENET**

I don't care why. Just fix it.

**GASTON**

Yes – yes I'll have to go back and get my toolbox right after we get this window opened. Okay you get over here and give me a hand.

> *GASTON places the crowbar against the windowsill.*

**PIERRE**

We already tried opening it there.

**GASTON**

Well let's try it again. Okay ready and.... *(They both apply pressure to the crowbar.)* It's coming... it's... ahhh come on baby, come on. *(GASTON grunts.)* It's coming. Ahhh.... *Merde!* Ahhh – Mother of God! *(GASTON pulls the crowbar away from the window and catches his breath.)* This place is going to be the death of me.

**PIERRE**

*(under his breath)* With any luck.

**GASTON**

I'm telling you if it were up to me I'd sell this eyesore and let them tear it down.

**PIERRE**

But it's not up to you, it's up to Mama.

**GASTON**

You're really asking for it today, you little punk.

**PIERRE**

I'm just stating the facts.

**GASTON**

Yeah, well as long as we're stating the facts, if it were up to me you'd be out on your ass like your friend Luc. Oh you think I didn't know his folks kicked him out, hein?

**PIERRE**

He doesn't care.

**GASTON**

Why should he when he can always put the squeeze on you when he needs cash?

**GENET**

Gentlemen, the window?

*GENET jots a note in the leopard notebook and then returns to the manuscript.*

**GASTON**

Okay, back to work, you. *(GASTON and PIERRE return to work.)* By the way, your mother told me about your "little strike threat." Go ahead, that'll just give us an excuse to hire someone who gives a shit that we're trying to run a business here.

**PIERRE**

Maybe you should turn it into a whorehouse.

**GASTON**

Hein?

**PIERRE**

The hotel. If you turned it into a whorehouse, then instead of working our backs to the bone you'd have a stable of employees to do it for us.

**GENET**

*(laughs)* Ha! Brilliant!

*GASTON pulls the crowbar from the window.*

**GASTON**

He's an idiot! Wait 'til your mother hears about this one.

**GENET**

Oh come on now, no reason to snitch on the boy just because he can give as good as he gets. (*The light flickers and then snaps out.*)

**GASTON**

Goddamn it!

> *A shaft of light streams in from the toilet doorway along with the sound of flamenco music and we are transported to the private parlour of Madame Petite's Barrio Chino Bordello in Barcelona, 1934. MARIANNE/MADAME PETITE enters. She walks over to the desk followed by the actor playing LUC in the role of the transvestite, LUMIA.*

**MARIANNE/MADAME PETITE**

It's busy out there tonight, Lumia, so I want you to stay away from the booze.

**LUC/LUMIA**

Yes, Madame Petite.

> *MARIANNE/MADAME PETITE turns on the lamp on the desk and notices PIERRE/YOUNG GENET and GASTON/STILITANO. GASTON/STILITANO has a crippled arm.*

**MARIANNE/MADAME PETITE**

Ah, we have guests.

**GENET**

Good evening, Madame Petite.

**PIERRE/YOUNG GENET**

Lumia...

**MARIANNE/MADAME PETITE**

Jean... Stilitano.

> *She sits at the desk and retouches her make-up.*

**PIERRE/YOUNG GENET**

Madame Petite, I seem to have gotten myself in a little fiduciary difficulty.

William Webster, Andrew Hachey, Maria Vacratsis and Ralph Small
*photo by David Hawe*

## GASTON/STILITANO

I don't know how many times I've told him to make sure the johns have cash on them before he brings them up to the room, the idiot! It doesn't take a genius to remember that. You tell the horny bastards if they have the cash they get to fuck your ass. If they don't, they get to fuck themselves.

**PIERRE/YOUNG GENET**

I did but he just kept buying me drinks and then by the time we got back to his room he had hardly any cash left. Stilitano, please don't be mad at me, you know it makes my heart bleed.

**GASTON/STILITANO**

If you don't come up with the rest of the money I'll make you bleed for real, you little faggot.

**PIERRE/YOUNG GENET**

Madame Petite, knowing that your legendary generosity is the only thing that rivals your great beauty… I was wondering if I might impose on your renowned largesse?

**MARIANNE/MADAME PETITE**

I'm sorry, Jean, but I haven't got a peseta on me.

**GENET**

A woman such as yourself without a peseta?

**MARIANNE/MADAME PETITE**

*(in a low voice)* Come 'round to my apartment later—

**GASTON/STILITANO**

You dragged me all the way over here and you still can't pay up? You're pathetic!

**LUC/LUMIA**

Stilitano, is that any way to talk to your girlfriend?

**GASTON/STILITANO**

Fuck you, you syphilitic cooze.

> GASTON/STILITANO *moves toward LUC/LUMIA, who stands her ground. PIERRE/YOUNG GENET puts himself between them.*

**PIERRE/YOUNG GENET**

No, leave Lumia alone; take it out on me if you have to.

**GASTON/STILITANO**

I would if I didn't know you'd get pleasure out of it.

**MARIANNE/MADAME PETITE**

I have a customer who would pay good money to hear this conversation.

**PIERRE/YOUNG GENET**

No matter how you've treated me / I'm not ashamed of the love I feel for you.

**GENET**

/ I'm not ashamed of the love I feel for you.

**GASTON/STILITANO**

You don't feel love for me. You feel lust for the monster that hangs between my legs. But you're wasting your time because I don't shove it up the asses of faggots.

**LUC/LUMIA**

Yet you spend more time in the company of faggots than women.

**PIERRE/YOUNG GENET**

Yeah, you might not shove it up our asses but you sure enjoy waving it in our faces.

> GASTON/STILITANO *raises his fist to strike*
> PIERRE/YOUNG GENET.

**MARIANNE/MADAME PETITE**

You hit him in here and I'll ban you from my house forever, Stilitano.

**GASTON/STILITANO**

This is between him and me—

**MARIANNE/MADAME PETITE**

And this is my house. / And in my house you'll follow my rules!

**GASTON/STILITANO**

/ You better stay out of this, woman—

**MARIANNE/MADAME PETITE**

Or you'll what? What? You'll smack me around like one of your whores who doesn't have the guts to fight back? You think I'm afraid of you? Fuck you! You're a cheap pimp with a bum arm and a big dick. You mess with me and we'll see who has the biggest dick of all!

**PIERRE/YOUNG GENET**

Don't provoke him, Madame Petite.

**MARIANNE/MADAME PETITE**

Oh, I know he's got a stiletto hidden in his boot. You just try and use that on me and I guarantee you'll never leave the Barrio Chino

Bordello alive. Honestly, Jean, I really don't know why you waste your time following this piece of trash around.

**PIERRE/YOUNG GENET**

We're partners.

**MARIANNE/MADAME PETITE**

Partners? Well has your "partner" told you about the fresh chicken he's grooming? Has he told you about the beautiful Roberto?

**GASTON/STILITANO**

You bitch.

**LUC/LUMIA**

Oooh, beautiful Roberto.

**MARIANNE/MADAME PETITE**

All right that's enough, Lumia, let's leave them to their business. And just remember, Stilitano if you hurt one hair on this boy's head, I won't rest until I have that "monument of masculinity" that you take such pride in floating in a pickle jar on my bar. *(They exit.)*

**GENET**

So?

**GASTON/STILITANO**

Look, why don't we forget about the rest of the money and call it even?

**PIERRE/YOUNG GENET**

Coward.

**GASTON/STILITANO**

Okay, this is the deal; you're getting a little long in the tooth to pull off the chicken bit with the old guys.

**PIERRE/YOUNG GENET**

I'm only twenty for fuck's sake.

**GASTON/STILITANO**

Yeah and you look like shit. The old queens want boys that look fresh and innocent and that's why I'm bringing Roberto into the deal.

**PIERRE/YOUNG GENET**

When were you going to tell me?

> *GASTON/STILITANO offers a noncommittal shrug of his shoulders.*

You know, Stilitano, maybe it would be better if I did step aside. We both know that a two-way split's better than three and...

**GENET**

You know how jealous I can get.

**GASTON/STILITANO**

Yeah well, you've been a real pal, Jean. No hard feelings?

**PIERRE/YOUNG GENET**

Actually... I've also got a new partner lined up.

**GASTON/STILITANO**

Oh?

**PIERRE/YOUNG GENET**

I found him at the Cabaret Criolla.

**GENET**

It's true Roberto is very beautiful.

**GASTON/STILITANO**

What have you done?

**PIERRE/YOUNG GENET**

Seems that we've both been keeping secrets... but I didn't keep any from Roberto.

**GASTON/STILITANO**

What did you tell him?

**PIERRE/YOUNG GENET**

How the cash would really be split if he partnered up with you.

**GASTON/STILITANO**

You backstabbing twat!

**PIERRE/YOUNG GENET**

After that it took no time at all to convince him that there might be more money to be had with a younger partner.

**GASTON/STILITANO**

I won't let you get away with this.

**PIERRE/YOUNG GENET**

But I already have. So like you said, no hard feelings?

**GASTON/STILITANO**

I'll kill you before I let you ruin me.

*GASTON/STILITANO pulls a stiletto out of his boot. He and PIERRE/YOUNG GENET begin to slowly circle each other as the sound of the flamenco music grows in volume.*

**GENET**

Ah, finally the infamous stiletto!

**PIERRE/YOUNG GENET**

Are you forgetting what Madame Petite said would happen if you used that on me?

**GASTON/STILITANO**

So that's why you brought me here? Because you knew she'd protect you? Well I'll stick that hag in the guts, too, if I have to.

**PIERRE/YOUNG GENET**

You have no idea how much I love you.

**GASTON/STILITANO**

This is how you show it?

**PIERRE/YOUNG GENET**

No, this is how I destroy it! *(He rips open his own shirt.)* Come on, one thrust straight through the heart. Do it! Do it, you bastard, do it! Do it – do it – do it! *(beat)* And you had the nerve to call me pathetic.

**GENET**

Madame Petite was right…

**PIERRE/YOUNG GENET**

You're nothing but lots of talk and lots of cock and that's about it.

**GASTON/STILITANO**

Jean, please don't do this.

**PIERRE/YOUNG GENET**

It's done.

**GENET**

And so are you.

**GASTON/STILITANO**

I could put an end to you, too, without sticking you with this if I let the cops know where that escaped convict they've been looking for has been hiding out.

**PIERRE/YOUNG GENET**

You'd squeal?

*GASTON/STILITANO nods.*

Then I'll bring you down with me.

**GENET**

Remember, I know where the body's buried.

**PIERRE/YOUNG GENET**

Now piss off before I let everybody know just what kind of pussy you really are.

*GASTON/STILITANO collects himself and exits. The lights go to black and we hear GENET laughing in the dark.*

**PIERRE**

What's so funny?

*GENET laughs.*

**GENET**

Pussy.

**PIERRE**

Not the ones I've seen.

*The lights flicker back on and we return to the present.*

**GENET**

How long have we been sitting here?

**PIERRE**

Uh… I don't know. Maybe three, four minutes?

**GENET**

Mmmm…. What happened to your father?

**PIERRE**

He went to check the fuse box, don't you remember?

**GENET**

Oh… yes, yes that's right.

**PIERRE**

You don't really remember, do you?

**GENET**

Oh, I remember…. But one has to be careful with memories because every pastoral trail you follow can lead to a very dark forest with sinkholes hidden along the way, covered in the softest moss. You see? / Hein you see?

**PIERRE**

What / – what? You don't trust them?

**GENET**

They're phantoms, chimeras! Beatific and demonic all distorted reflections. They're a trap! Mental flypaper! *(He stares off into space. Beat.)*

**PIERRE**

Monsieur?

**GENET**

And then yet again… they can be useful…. Out of the fog an old trick emerges… that used to come in handy. A-ha!

> *GENET reaches into his pocket and removes a small penknife. He walks over to the window while exposing the blade. He inserts the knife blade between one side of the windowsill and window frame and scrapes the knife along the narrow space between window frame and sill.*

You don't want old paint getting in the way of a quick escape.

> *He quickly repeats the procedure on the other side of the window.*

Try it now.

> *PIERRE braces himself at the window and prepares to open it. Then, with very little effort, the window opens.*

Ah, there we go.

**PIERRE**

You mean you could have done that all along?

**GENET**

Oh, did I forget the final indignity memory inflicts? It abandons you when you need it most just like a faithless lover. *(beat)*

**PIERRE**

I better get going before the tyrant gets back. See you.

> *PIERRE moves to exit. GENET returns to the desk.*

**GENET**

You'd best keep your wits about you, Pierre, because tyrants…
*(GASTON enters)* come in many guises.

**GASTON**

Where do you think you're going?

**PIERRE**

To meet Luc.

**GASTON**

What about…?

**PIERRE**

The window? Check it out.

**GASTON**

You got it open. How?

**PIERRE**

Who cares how? It's open, just back off—

**GASTON**

What did you just say to me?

**PIERRE**

It's open – it's open! / What the fuck – I'm getting out of here.

*GASTON grabs PIERRE by the arm.*

**GASTON**

/ Repeat what you said—

**PIERRE**

I said… *(He shakes himself loose and runs off.)* you're an asshole!

**GASTON**

Son of a bitch! You'll have to come back sooner or later! You just wait!

**GENET**

At least he got it open.

**GASTON**

Well, he's usually pretty useless around here.

**GENET**

Still, he's your son and you have to—

**GASTON**

If he were my son he wouldn't have turned out like this, little bastard.

**GENET**

If?

**GASTON**

What?

**GENET**

You said "if" he were your son.

**GASTON**

Oh…. I just meant… if… he acted… more like a son… he uh…

**GENET**

*(in a low voice)* He's not really your kid, is he?

**GASTON**

Uh…

**GENET**

*(in a low voice)* He doesn't look much like you. *(GASTON shakes his head.)* He doesn't know? *(GASTON shakes his head again.)*

**GENET**

*(in a low voice)* How long have you had him?

**GASTON**

*(in a low voice)* Since he was two. It's complicated…. Marianne's family's involved…. They wanted it to be kept secret.

**GENET**

*(in a low voice)* Oh I see, you took him in under duress.

**GASTON**

*(in a low voice)* Either that or put him up for adoption.

**GENET**

*(in a low voice)* And your wife couldn't bear to see the little waif cast off so you were saddled with someone else's kid? *(GASTON nods. GENET's voice returns to normal volume.)* Well, we all have our crosses to bear, my friend, and now I must return to mine. You see, Gaston, the most insulting thing you can do to words, is ignore them.

**GASTON**

Words mean a lot to you, huh?

**GENET**

They're all I have left.

> *GASTON exits. GENET jots down some notes in the leopard notebook and then returns to his manuscript. The sound of Parisian jazz circa 1940 is heard softly playing as the lighting transforms from late afternoon to the dead of night. Exhausted, GENET takes the pills from his pocket and downs a couple with a glass of water. He leaves the manuscript on the desk and crosses over to the bed and lies down.*

> *Blackout.*

## SCENE FOUR

> *Lights come up on a posh hotel room, Paris circa 1940. PIERRE/YOUNG GENET pulls himself through the window. His partner, NONO, played by the actor in the role of LUC, waits on the street below.*

**LUC/NONO**

So, is anybody home?

**PIERRE/YOUNG GENET**

*(loud whispering)* Shhhh, not so loud.

> *LUC/NONO climbs through the window.*

**LUC/NONO**

*(loud whispering)* So is he here or isn't he? Neither of us can afford to go in front of a judge again, Jean. They'll put us away for good if we get caught—

**PIERRE/YOUNG GENET**

We're not going to get caught, Nono, because I arranged to meet the guy who lives here at his favourite spot in the Place Pigalle for a night of absinthe and reefer. He's sitting there right now waiting for me to arrive. Probably taking his first sip of absinthe even as we speak so he's not going to mind it too much when I show up half an hour late.

> *PIERRE/YOUNG GENET closes the window and shutters. He turns on the lamp on the desk.*

**LUC/NONO**

Okay, so who is this guy and what are we after?

**PIERRE/YOUNG GENET**
He's just this rich guy who bought one of my poems.

**LUC/NONO**
No kidding? How much he give you?

**PIERRE/YOUNG GENET**
Obviously not enough.

**LUC/NONO**
So what are we looking for?

**PIERRE/YOUNG GENET**
Books.

**LUC/NONO**
Books? You're yanking me, no seriously, Jean, what are we looking for?

**PIERRE/YOUNG GENET**
Books.

**LUC/NONO**
What the fuck are we going to do with books? I hate books—

**PIERRE/YOUNG GENET**
Nono, calm down—

**LUC/NONO**
No, you calm down – you calm down – I don't even see any books!
Who gives a shit about books?

**PIERRE/YOUNG GENET**
Nono, if you don't shut up the / neighbours are going to call the cops—

**LUC/NONO**
*(loud whispering)* / Are they made of gold?

**PIERRE/YOUNG GENET**
/ No—

**LUC/NONO**
Then why the hell / would we want to steal them?

**PIERRE/YOUNG GENET**
/ Shhhh—

**LUC/NONO**
/ People are beginning to talk, Jean—

**PIERRE/YOUNG GENET**

Oh yeah?

**LUC/NONO**

You've been acting differently since you've been hanging out with these "rich artsy type" friends of yours.

**PIERRE/YOUNG GENET**

No I haven't. It's just that you guys are a bunch of jealous lug heads.

**LUC/NONO**

No, that's not it – it's – well some of the guys think it's kind of queer that you write poems.

**PIERRE/YOUNG GENET**

What's it to you if I am? We're just doing a job.

**LUC/NONO**

What's it going to look like when the boys ask me what we got in the haul and I tell them we stole a bunch of goddamn books?

**PIERRE/YOUNG GENET**

Not a bunch, only three. *(He goes to the bed, reaches underneath it, and retrieves a small box.)* Three very, very special rare first editions.

**LUC/NONO**

Books are boring unless... they're sexy? What do you call it – pornographic? You know what I mean...?

**PIERRE/YOUNG GENET**

*(sighs)* Sorry to disappoint you, Nono, but they're philosophical not pornographic.

**LUC/NONO**

So what are we going to do with them?

**PIERRE/YOUNG GENET**

Read them, sell them, and then eat.

**LUC/NONO**

Read them? I have to read them? Are you nuts? You see that's what I'm talking about, Jean—

**PIERRE/YOUNG GENET**

I'll read them, I'll sell them, and then we'll eat.

*He lifts a small antique book out of the box.*

**LUC/NONO**
Why do you have to read them first when we're starving?

**PIERRE/YOUNG GENET**
Because the words will feed me for a lifetime.

**LUC/NONO**
I just don't get you, Jean. You didn't need me to come on this job with you. You knew the place was going to be empty, hell you even knew where he hid them. So why did you ask me to come along?

**PIERRE/YOUNG GENET**
I knew you could use something to eat.

**LUC/NONO**
So could a lot of guys, why me?

> *GENET gets up from the bed.*

**GENET**
I like to watch you eat.

**LUC/NONO**
You – you like to watch me eat?

**PIERRE/YOUNG GENET**
One night after a job I watched you tear a chicken apart and suck the meat off every bone and as I watched you devour that bird whole…

**GENET**
I wished it were me.

**LUC/NONO**
You want me?

> *GENET steps into the scene.*

**PIERRE/YOUNG GENET**
I want to step inside of you…

**GENET**
And see the avatar of love's incarnations reflected in haunted echoes…

**PIERRE/YOUNG GENET**
I want to breathe you…

**GENET**
Lucien…

Dan Watson, William Webster and Andrew Hachey
*photo by David Hawe*

**PIERRE/YOUNG GENET**
I want to taste you…

**GENET**
Jean Decarnin…

**PIERRE/YOUNG GENET**
I want to adorn you with a garland of kisses…

**GENET**
Java…

**PIERRE/YOUNG GENET**
I want to worship at the temple you inhabit…

**GENET**
Abdallah…

**PIERRE/YOUNG GENET**

I want to sacrifice myself on the altar of your beauty...

**GENET**

Mohammed...

**PIERRE/YOUNG GENET**

I want my martyrdom to grant me access to Elysium where the blessed dead are reunited for eternity.

**GENET**

It's love, pal, that's what I want, that's all it ever was for me, and even though you're one of many... *(He steps out of the scene and returns to the bed.)*

**PIERRE/YOUNG GENET**

In this moment you're the only one.

**LUC/NONO**

Okay, I'll let you blow me here if you promise to read fast.

> *PIERRE/YOUNG GENET kneels before LUC/NONO and puts the box of books down. He smiles and reaches for LUC/NONO's zipper, however before he can open it, the sound of loud footsteps are heard approaching down the hallway toward the door.*

Shit!

> *PIERRE/YOUNG GENET and LUC/NONO make a hasty retreat out through the window.*

> *Blackout.*

## SCENE FIVE

> *Early the next morning. The sound of distant city traffic is heard. Morning light streams through the window revealing GENET, sleeping on the bed in the same clothes from the night before. There is a knock and we hear MARIANNE's voice offstage.*

**MARIANNE**

*(offstage)* Monsieur, Monsieur are you awake?

**GENET**

    *(stirs)* Um?

**MARIANNE**

    *(offstage)* Monsieur it's very important that I talk to you.

        *More knocking. GENET sits up.*

**GENET**

    Yes, yes, you don't have to knock the door down.

**MARIANNE**

    We've been robbed.

        *GENET gets up and lets MARIANNE into the room.*

**GENET**

    What? When?

**MARIANNE**

    Last night. Some of the other guests reported things stolen and I wanted to check and see if anything of yours was missing.

        *GENET goes over to the desk drawer and opens it.*

**GENET**

    My wallet's gone.

**MARIANNE**

    Anything else?

**GENET**

    I don't have anything else of any value except… *(He glances over to the place on the desk where he left the manuscript the night before.)* My manuscript. *(He searches the desk frantically. He looks around the room.)* It's gone! My manuscript! Some bastard's stolen my manuscript!

        *Blackout.*

        *End of Act One.*

# ACT TWO

## SCENE ONE

*Lights come up on GENET and MARIANNE in the same positions they occupied at the end of Act One.*

**GENET**
My manuscript! That was the final draft—

**MARIANNE**
You don't have a copy?

*GENET reacts to a spasm of pain in his throat.*

**GENET**
Ahhh—

**MARIANNE**
Monsieur you're not well…. Do you need a doctor?

*GENET gets his pills and takes a couple.*

**GENET**
No, no none of that. I have no time. I have to get my manuscript back.

**MARIANNE**
But what if… if anything should happen… who should we call? Do you have family?

**GENET**
Family?

**MARIANNE**
Loved ones?

**GENET**
I love those who I loved, and I have already ensured their immortality. *(beat)* Don't worry, Madame, my bill shall not go unpaid.

**MARIANNE**
No – no, Monsieur, I'm not worried about that…

**GENET**
Yes, we've got other things to worry about at the moment.

**MARIANNE**
I've already called the police and they're on their way.

**GENET**

And a lot of good they'll do. Who else was hit?

**MARIANNE**

Everyone on your floor. Room three is missing his passport and wallet. Room five is also missing his wallet, watch and personal jewellery. Oh, and the Canadian in room nine, she had jewellery, credit cards and travellers cheques. All gone.

**GENET**

Where was Pierre while all this was happening?

**MARIANNE**

Asleep in bed until Gaston woke him up a few minutes ago.

**GENET**

What did he do last night?

**MARIANNE**

Nothing, came home early and stayed in.

**GENET**

On a Saturday night? *(beat)* Don't you find that odd? To bed early on a Saturday night?

**MARIANNE**

What are you getting at, Monsieur?

**GENET**

Pierre introduced me to his friend Luc yesterday… I noticed a little hero worship going on.

**MARIANNE**

Yes.

**GENET**

Love and money are the two things that can make even the smartest people bend to the will of others, Madame… and Luc needs money.

**MARIANNE**

Are you suggesting…?

**GENET**

Breaking and entering is a cash and carry business. Cash, credit cards, passports and jewellery, that all makes sense. Even gold teeth and a glass eye would fit the profile but a worthless bunch of papers scribbled on by an old man? I can assure you from personal experience, Madame, that no professional, no matter how adept, could have pulled this off so seamlessly without some help from the inside.

**MARIANNE**

But.... Oh my God – oh my God, what if you're right?

**GENET**

If I am, Pierre's gotten himself in a serious bit of trouble.

**MARIANNE**

No, he wouldn't dare.

**GENET**

But what about Luc?

**MARIANNE**

I'll just go and settle this right now and ask Pierre to his face. I can always tell when he's lying. *(She moves to exit.)*

**GENET**

And if he is then Gaston will get involved, then the cops, and then it'll be out of our hands. Luc's probably holding the goods. If Pierre gets caught there's a possibility Luc will panic and ditch the stuff and I'll never see my manuscript again.

**MARIANNE**

But Monsieur, if Pierre's broken the law I have legal responsibilities – I—

**GENET**

Do you want to see Pierre get arrested? Do you? Do you want to see him go in front of a judge and face real prison time?

> *The sound of jail cell doors slamming shut is heard as PIERRE/YOUNG GENET is revealed standing in a prisoner's dock. The window shutters swing open revealing the JUDGE, played by the actor in the role of GASTON, sitting in a judge's chair.*

**GASTON/JUDGE**

*(severely)* So, you're a thief. Caught red-handed in the owner's house stealing three rare antique books.

**GENET**

Jewellery, passports, credit cards, my manuscript, this isn't kid's stuff.

**GASTON/JUDGE**

What were you going to do with them? Eh?

**MARIANNE**

Monsieur, I'm completely aware of the seriousness of the situation.

**GASTON/JUDGE**

You certainly weren't going to read them. Ha!

**MARIANNE**

It was you yourself who suggested—

**GASTON/JUDGE**

You're a thief, and you were going to sell them, weren't you?

**MARIANNE**

I should at least talk to Gaston—

**GENET**

No – no – no, haven't you been listening?

**GASTON/JUDGE**

Tell me, my child; please tell me you're a thief.

**GENET**

If you confront him with this and he is involved, first he'll deny—

**PIERRE/YOUNG GENET**

But I'm innocent.

**GENET**

Then confess.

**GASTON/JUDGE**

And tears, don't forget the tears. I want to see tears gushing from those lying eyes. The power of tears!

**GENET**

And then he'll promise to repent but it'll be too late because then Gaston – Gaston! Well I think we both know what Gaston's reaction will be.

**MARIANNE**

But if you think Pierre and Luc stole your manuscript and you want it back—

**GASTON/JUDGE**

Oh, come on now. Don't tell me you're new at this?

**GENET**

You just have to ask yourself if you want to see Pierre's future go down the toilet? Because that's what you've got to be prepared to face if he's involved. Not to mention the reputation of your fine establishment.

**GASTON/JUDGE**

Don't you know how it works?

**PIERRE/YOUNG GENET**

No!

**MARIANNE**

I raised him to have respect for rules… for the law. He knows the difference between right and wrong…

**GENET**

Good for him. See what good it does him when he's standing in front of a judge who's seen dozens just like him.

**GASTON/JUDGE**

You look familiar, have I seen you in my courtroom before?

*PIERRE/YOUNG GENET shakes his head.*

**GENET**

To the judge he'll look just like any other recalcitrant little thief dolled up for his day in court. Then the judge will perform his function and Pierre will be assigned his.

**GASTON/JUDGE**

I want you to understand that you, the law, and I are inextricably bound together.

**GENET**

You see, Madame, we all have our functions that bind us together under the law.

**MARIANNE**

Functions?

**GASTON/JUDGE**

Yes, because without thieves there would be no need for laws.

**GENET**

My function, in the eyes of the law, is to play the helpless victim of theft demanding justice.

**GASTON/JUDGE**

Without laws there would be no need for judges.

**GENET**

Your function? The negligent, shame-filled mother.

**GASTON/JUDGE**

Without judges thousands upon thousands of lawyers' lives would be ruined! Could you imagine? No – you have to be a model thief if I'm going to be a model judge. If you become a fake thief then I become a fake judge and that would make a mockery of the law!

**GENET**

Do you understand now?

**GASTON/JUDGE**

There must be thieves so I can demonstrate my authority.

**MARIANNE**

I was never a negligent mother.

**GENET**

(*As GENET talks he becomes more impassioned.*) Of course not. And a thief is not just a thief. But as far as the law is concerned we all must perform our functions in order to maintain the status quo! An ever-changing phantasmagoria of leading characters playing the same roles over and over again in different drag!

**GASTON/JUDGE**

/ Order—

*GENET crosses over to his desk.*

**GENET**

/ But in the end all their promises of *Liberté, Fraternité, Égalité* go up in smoke like a cheap magician's trick!

*He throws the stack of papers on the desk into the air.*

**GASTON/JUDGE**

/ Order—

**MARIANNE**

/ Monsieur, please calm down—

**GENET**

And when the smoke clears all that's left are the ruined remains that hypocrisy, corruption and avarice have wrought.

**GASTON/JUDGE**

I said order in the court!

**MARIANNE**

That all might be very true, Monsieur, but making a mess of this room isn't going to help matters.

**GASTON/JUDGE**

*(pointing to GENET)* Are you the young man's lawyer? Wait a minute I know you. I've seen your face in my courtroom plenty of times. You're nothing but a petty thief yourself. And not a very good one as I recall. Always getting caught and for what? Prostitution, carrying an illegal weapon, stealing books, bolts of fabric…

**GENET**

Food.

**MARIANNE**

I'm sorry, Monsieur I haven't had time to think of preparing breakfast…

**GENET**

I'm not hungry.

**MARIANNE**

But you just said…

> *The JUDGE pulls out a long scroll and unfurls it.*

**GASTON/JUDGE**

It says here, "public ward-number 192.102," that you were discharged from the army for reasons of "mental imbalance" and "A-morality."

**GENET**

"They do not sin at all who sin for love."

**MARIANNE**

Monsieur you're not making any sense.

**GASTON/JUDGE**

A psychiatrist finally examined you after one of your numerous arrests…

**MARIANNE**

I think the strain of losing your manuscript has been a little too much for you.

**GASTON/JUDGE**

And came to the conclusion that you suffer from a "delicate constitution and a weak mind."

**GENET**

There's nothing wrong with my mind, it's just that I've seen the kind of havoc the judicial system can inflict on a young man's life. *(He begins to cry.)* I can't bear the thought of you and Pierre having to endure it.

**GASTON/JUDGE**

Finally the tears!

**MARIANNE**

No, Monsieur, please don't cry…. If anyone should be crying it should be me. *(She begins to cry.)* Oh, Monsieur, what am I going to do? The police are going to be here any minute.

**GENET**

*(recovering quickly)* Maybe there's another way.

**GASTON/JUDGE**

There will be a brief recess while the court considers its verdict.

*The shutters on the windows close as the lights on PIERRE/YOUNG GENET fade to black.*

**MARIANNE**

I'm sorry, Monsieur, I can't think of anything.

**GENET**

I think we should try to find out for ourselves if Pierre had anything to do with it. If we discover that he was involved then maybe we can convince him to come clean, return the stolen goods, and avoid being arrested.

**MARIANNE**

But how?

**GENET**

Have you told Pierre what was stolen from each of the rooms?

**MARIANNE**

Not yet.

**GENET**

Good. Then here's what I want you to do. When you report to the cops what's been stolen tell them about everything that's missing except for my manuscript and wallet. The same goes for Pierre and Gaston.

**MARIANNE**

But won't I be breaking the law if I don't report it to the police?

**GENET**

I don't see how, after all it is my property and it's my prerogative to report the theft or not, and I choose not to. All you have to do is go to the front desk and wait for the cops with Gaston. When they arrive co-operate with them fully and give them any information they request, omitting my missing items. I'm going to go out and do a few errands and then later this afternoon once the dust has settled I want you to send Pierre to my room for a pickup and delivery and then leave the rest to me.

**MARIANNE**

Oh. Monsieur I'm scared, I'm worried for Pierre.

**GENET**

You have every reason to be. However if you can put your trust in me, we may be able to avert disaster.

**MARIANNE**

I don't seem to have much choice.

**GENET**

Oh, but you do. *(beat)*

**MARIANNE**

I'll send him up around three-thirty.

**GENET**

I'll be sure to let you know if I find out anything.

**MARIANNE**

Thank you for your kindness, Monsieur.

> *She exits. GENET quickly begins to collect the paper strewn around the room. The window shutters open revealing GASTON/JUDGE in his chair.*

**GASTON/JUDGE**

The court has reached a verdict.

**GENET**

Save it for someone who gives a shit.

*GENET continues to straighten up the room.*

**GASTON/JUDGE**

After due consideration of the facts that have been put before me including the present offence, past convictions, un-served sentences, and reported mental state I am compelled to sentence the defendant to life imprisonment.

*GENET suffers another attack of pain in his throat. PIERRE/YOUNG GENET reappears in the prisoner's dock.*

**GENET**

No, not now – I don't have time for this now! Ahhh!

*GENET hunts for his pills and then quickly gobbles a couple and collapses on the bed waiting for them to take effect.*

**PIERRE/YOUNG GENET**

Life imprisonment? No, there must be some mistake!

*The actor playing LUC enters with theatrical flare in the role of Jean COCTEAU.*

**LUC/COCTEAU**

My lord, I beg you to stay that sentence.

**GASTON/JUDGE**

The court recognizes Monsieur Jean Cocteau.

**LUC/COCTEAU**

Take care, my lord; this is a great writer, perhaps one of the greatest of our time.

**GASTON/JUDGE**

Him, that pipsqueak?

**LUC/COCTEAU**

Don't appraise him by his uncouth appearance, my lord. It was a mistake I made myself when this "convict poet" first arrived at my doorstep with a manuscript he had written in prison on scrap pieces of paper. Very intriguing. "Master," that's what he called me, "Master, I'd like to read you passages from my manuscript." And the defendant, standing, read for an hour from his first novel, *Our Lady of the*

*Flowers.* He read well, unaffectedly, with a rather astonishing assurance since he was, after all, facing me, Cocteau.

**GASTON/JUDGE**

Was it any good?

**LUC/COCTEAU**

I'll admit to you that at first while he was reading I didn't much like all those stories about drag queens. But I asked him to leave the manuscript so I could read the whole thing, and I found within it three hundred incredible pages in which he pieces together the mythology of queers.

**GASTON/JUDGE**

Queers?

**LUC/COCTEAU**

Yes, queers, thugs, beauty and death. Astonishing! Obscene flowers scented with divine decadence. Its very newness was unsettling. What was I to do? One dreams of possessing such a book and making it famous. But it belonged to another. What was I to do? I read it again that very night, line by line. I found everything in it hateful and worthy of respect. What was I to do with this book that was so extraordinary, obscure, unpublishable, inevitable? I considered the advice of a close confidant to burn it… but to burn it would have been too simple. It burns me. And if I burned it, it would burn me all the more because it is miraculous.

**GASTON/JUDGE**

Monsieur Cocteau, you are more knowledgeable than I in matters of art and literature, however I find it hard to believe that this creature would be capable of achieving the miraculous. His psychiatric report suggests he's practically an idiot with immature compulsive tendencies. *(He addresses PIERRE/YOUNG GENET.)* What would you say if someone stole this book you wrote?

**PIERRE/YOUNG GENET**

I would be proud of it.

**GASTON/JUDGE**

Proud? Do you know how much the books you tried to steal are worth?

**PIERRE/YOUNG GENET**

I don't know their actual monetary worth but I know their true value.

**LUC/COCTEAU**

My lord, the defendant's present state of poverty forced him into a desperate act but I can assure you that he is destined to be one of the brightest lights in France's literary firmament. *(He removes a letter from his pocket and gives it to the JUDGE.)* "My lord, we are aware the marginality of his work prevents its open distribution but the profundity of his talent compels us to ask you to pardon this very great poet. Please accept, my lord, the assurance of our gratitude and our feelings of deep respect. Signed, Jean-Paul Sartre and Jean Cocteau."

**GASTON/JUDGE**

Monsieur Cocteau, this is highly irregular.

**LUC/COCTEAU**

Not really, my lord, the cases of the poets Villon and Verlaine...

**GASTON/JUDGE**

Ah yes, of course, Villon and Verlaine, Mmm... *(beat)* The defendant will rise.

> *PIERRE/YOUNG GENET steps forward. GENET sits up on the bed.*

Given the extraordinary evidence lauded in your defence by these distinguished character witnesses we have decided to reconsider our original sentence. And although this court can't annul your guilt we can revoke your life sentence with a full pardon under two conditions. One, that you never darken this courtroom with your presence again. And two, that you pay a fine of twenty thousand francs. This court is adjourned. *(The JUDGE's window shutters close.)*

**LUC/COCTEAU**

Congratulations, darling, you're a free man!

**GENET**

*(The drugs have begun to ease the pain.)* A fine of twenty thousand francs is hardly free.

**LUC/COCTEAU**

Now, Jean, we all know there's no need for you to steal anymore. You think I don't know that you sold the manuscript of Querelle for fifty thousand francs? And the sales for *The Thief's Journal* and *Miracle of the Rose* are going through the roof. No, now stealing is just a childhood habit that must be put aside for greater things.

**PIERRE/YOUNG GENET**

But how will I dream up new things to write about if I give up my life of crime?

**LUC/COCTEAU**

Listen you little brat, you just pay that fine and behave yourself. *(PIERRE/YOUNG GENET sticks his tongue out at him and exits.)* Don't be an ingrate. Sartre and I put our reputations on the line for you today.

**GENET**

You're both more than aware that your participation in today's events will become one of the cornerstones of my mythology and for that alone it's worth the risk.

**LUC/COCTEAU**

You're incorrigible, but brilliant. Sartre's expecting you for drinks at the Café de Flore. He'll want to hear your maniacally twisted perspective on the outcome of today's proceedings. Oh my, look at the time!

**GENET**

The time! What time is it? I've got to get things ready—

**LUC/COCTEAU**

Aha, did you line up some hot rough trade to celebrate your liberation?

**GENET**

Pierre.

**LUC/COCTEAU**

I'm sure he's absolutely dishy. Now I must fly, Man Ray is photographing my hands today! Good luck, *mon cherie*, and please stay out of trouble.

> COCTEAU *exits and the room returns to the present. After a beat* GENET *stands and puts on his jacket. He puts the bottle of pills in his jacket pocket and exits.*
>
> *Blackout.*

## SCENE TWO

*Late afternoon the same day. Lights come up on GENET sitting at the desk writing in his leopard notebook. There is a knock on the door.*

**GENET**

Yes?

**PIERRE**

It's Pierre.

**GENET**

Come in, it's open.

*PIERRE enters. GENET continues to write.*

**PIERRE**

You have something you want delivered?

*GENET looks up from his notebook.*

**GENET**

Um? Oh yes, just give me a minute. *(He puts the notebook down and crosses to the desk. He picks up a large envelope from the desk and puts a manuscript into it.)* I heard about the robberies that took place last night.

**PIERRE**

You heard...?

*GENET closes the envelope, but does not seal it, and proceeds to write an address on it.*

**GENET**

Yes, it's terrible isn't it? Your mother told me all about it. Did you have anything stolen?

**PIERRE**

Uh... my Walkman.

**GENET**

Oh, that's too bad. I heard the cops were here, too.

**PIERRE**

Yeah.

**GENET**

Do they have any ideas how the thief got in?

**PIERRE**
Through the basement window.

**GENET**
Ah.

> *GENET finishes writing the address on the envelope and hands it to PIERRE.*

Anyway, here you go. I finally finished my manuscript and I want you to deliver it to my publisher immediately.

> *PIERRE looks at the envelope in his hands.*

Something wrong?

**PIERRE**
Hein? Uh… no uh…

**GENET**
Oh, I know what I'm forgetting.

> *GENET reaches into the inner pocket of his jacket hanging over the back of the chair. He takes his wallet out, removes a couple of bills, and hands them to PIERRE. PIERRE stares dumfounded at the money and envelope.*

And there's a little something for your trouble. *(beat)* What, not enough? *(He gives PIERRE a couple more bills.)* Okay, okay I don't want you telling people I'm cheap, but that's it.

**PIERRE**
Uh… no um… you weren't robbed?

**GENET**
What would I have that would be of any value to a thief besides the few francs I keep in my wallet?

**PIERRE**
But—

**GENET**
Yes? *(beat)* You know I was so enchanted by you on that day we discussed writing that I decided to dedicate my book to you.

**PIERRE**
To me?

**GENET**

Open it and see.

> *PIERRE opens the unsealed envelope, pulls out the cover page, and looks at it in disbelief. Written in large letters on the sheet of paper are the words "Caught you!"*

What's the matter, don't you like it?

**PIERRE**

It says "caught you," is this some kind of joke?

> *PIERRE crumbles the cover page into a ball and throws it to the floor.*

**GENET**

Was it Luc?

**PIERRE**

What?

**GENET**

Was it Luc?

**PIERRE**

What are saying? Are you accusing Luc of robbing you? Is that it?

**GENET**

Was I robbed?

**PIERRE**

You're fucking with me.

**GENET**

Oh really? I thought it was the other way around.

**PIERRE**

You must be losing it, old man, because I don't know what you're talking about.

**GENET**

I was asking about the kiss.

**PIERRE**

Kiss?

**GENET**

The guy you kissed. Was it Luc? Well? Was it? *(beat)* Ah, sweet silence...

**PIERRE**

How the fuck did you…?

**GENET**

I'm psychic.

**PIERRE**

You're full of shit.

**GENET**

Want me to prove it? Want me to tell you how your heart burns with desire when his quick temper shoots thunderbolts through it? How his wicked laugh fills it with joy? How his most casual gaze holds it; hanging by arteries transformed into vines, clinging to the overripe fruit that once pumped blood but now drips love.

**PIERRE**

You fucking faggot.

**GENET**

Have I looked too deeply into the locket of your heart, tough guy?

**PIERRE**

You don't know what the fuck you're talking about, you fucking pervert.

**GENET**

You can shower me with spit if you like. But be warned, in that act of humiliation the stings of your venom will cascade through my being like warm honey.

**PIERRE**

You're fucking nuts.

**GENET**

Come on, you can do better than that. *(PIERRE moves to exit.)* I see. Now the hasty retreat. Coward.

**PIERRE**

Watch your mouth, old man.

**GENET**

Or what? You'll finish me off? *(He grabs PIERRE.)* Go ahead. At this moment I can think of no better way to die than at the hands of an enraged beauty. If it was good enough for Pasolini, it's good enough for me.

*PIERRE frees himself from GENET's grip.*

**PIERRE**

I'm not a faggot.

**GENET**

I don't give a shit what you think you are. I just know that you can't wait to feel Luc's warm lips devouring yours again.

**PIERRE**

Stop it—

**GENET**

His hot breath and hungry tongue—

**PIERRE**

No—

**GENET**

Then you hated it?

**PIERRE**

No—

**GENET**

You didn't hate it?

**PIERRE**

I didn't feel anything.

**GENET**

You felt everything.

**PIERRE**

Why are you doing this, hein? Are you trying to drive me crazy? What do you want? *(He begins to unzip his pants.)* You want to suck my cock? Is that what it's going to take to shut you up?

**GENET**

Put that away unless you intend to kill me with it. I can barely swallow spit without gagging. So who kissed who? Come on, you little closet case, who kissed who?

**PIERRE**

I'm not—

**GENET**

WHO KISSED WHO?!

**PIERRE**
Shhhh! – We were drunk…

**GENET**
Do you get drunk together often?

**PIERRE**
You going to jerk off over this when I leave?

**GENET**
What do you care? So who initiated? Him? *(beat)*

**PIERRE**
Yes.

**GENET**
And you willingly complied? *(PIERRE nods.)* And then?

**PIERRE**
I don't remember.

**GENET**
Bullshit! That moment is etched on your lips, mind and soul forever. You can try to convince yourself that it never happened but like the murderer who has buried his dirty work in a far off desolate place it'll come back to haunt you in your dreams.

**PIERRE**
No, I… I don't want to… I don't want to forget.

**GENET**
Why should you?

**PIERRE**
Because it's impossible…. It's…. For him it's in the moment, it's animal, he doesn't care if it's a guy or girl, he just wants to get off and…

**GENET**
For you it's something else?

**PIERRE**
I tried to convince myself that it was nothing. But then it happened again.

**GENET**
And again, and again, and again? *(PIERRE nods.)* Beyond kisses to full consummation?

**PIERRE**

I won't let him fuck me.

**GENET**

But you'd help him steal from your own family.

**PIERRE**

His family's cut him off okay? And he's totally broke and—

**GENET**

You couldn't bear to see him suffer.

**PIERRE**

It's just a bad scene for him right now.

**GENET**

So he came up with an idea on how to make some quick cash?

**PIERRE**

We're going to get out of here. He's got friends in Greece he can stay with.

**GENET**

You're eloping. How romantic. And to Greece, how appropriate.

**PIERRE**

No, it's not like that. I just need to get out of here. I haven't told him yet, but I'll go nuts if I have to spend another day following Gaston around here trying to keep this dump from falling apart. And as much as I love Mama, living with her is like living under the pope's skirt. It's time to go.

**GENET**

Not before you return my manuscript.

**PIERRE**

Manuscript?

**GENET**

Don't play me for a stupid bitch! This is the real deal – so you better listen carefully, because you're about to make the most important decision of you life. Now I don't care what you do with the rest of your haul but the return of my manuscript is imperative and non-negotiable. Failure to return it to me will result in a permanent postponement of your little honeymoon.

**PIERRE**

So what are you going to do? Tell my mother, Gaston, the police? You think I'm afraid of them?

**GENET**

I'll have you and Luc killed.

**PIERRE**

What?

**GENET**

You heard me. I'll have you both killed. I'm already a dead man so I have nothing to lose except that which you've taken from me. You however, have your whole life ahead of you – and believe me, when I say that if you cross me, the only trip you two will be taking will be to the morgue.

**PIERRE**

You're serious?

**GENET**

If you'd ever read one of my books, then you'd know that I'm well acquainted with the kind of people who will track you down and split you open for a very reasonable fee. You do have another option, of course. You could go to Marianne and Gaston and tell them that I've threatened your life. But then they'd want to know why. *(beat)* Would you mind picking that up and throwing it in the wastepaper basket? *(PIERRE picks up the crumpled piece of paper and throws it in the basket.)* Now tell me…. Why did Luc take it?

**PIERRE**

After he met you he wanted to check out if your story was true. So the next day we went to a Gallimard Bookstore…

**GENET**

And?

**PIERRE**

We stole a couple of your books, the ones about Spain and Mettray…. Everything you said was true. So when I told Luc that you were working on a new book right in our hotel… he was going to contact your publisher and…

**GENET**

Extort money for its safe return? *(PIERRE nods.)* I've got to give the little prick credit for trying. Very enterprising, but now bring it back to me before I have both of you strung up and quartered.

**PIERRE**

But— *(beat)* Okay.

**GENET**

I expect to have it in my hands by nine tonight or I'll set my dogs on you, understood?

> *PIERRE nods and exits. GENET crosses to the desk and writes in the leopard notebook.*
>
> *Blackout.*

## SCENE THREE

> *Early evening the same day. The sound of city traffic is heard, as the glow of streetlights streams through the window revealing GENET dozing on the windowsill. Suddenly there is a sharp gust of wind and the actress playing MARIANNE in the role of Simone DE BEAUVOIR arrives through the window. She looks down at and plops a folded newspaper into his lap. He wakes up with a start.*

**GENET**

Huh? Pierre?

**MARIANNE/DE BEAUVOIR**

Sorry to disappoint you, darling.

**GENET**

Simone? What the hell are you doing here?

**MARIANNE/DE BEAUVOIR**

Does one need a reason to visit an old friend?

**GENET**

When one hasn't spoken to the "old friend" for decades. It makes one curious as to the reason why Simone de Beauvoir herself should arrive at one's window casement. How did you find me?

> *MARIANNE/DE BEAUVOIR steps into the room.*

**MARIANNE/DE BEAUVOIR**

Oh, I have my ways.

**GENET**

Indeed you do and I find all of them irritating. So why don't you just spread your bat wings and go back where you came from.

**MARIANNE/DE BEAUVOIR**

Jean, is it really me you find so irritating, or the corner into which you've painted yourself?

**GENET**

Simone I'd rather have you sit on my face with that crusty old thing of yours than listen to you sermonize—

**MARIANNE/DE BEAUVOIR**

Why? Because you can't face the fact that you've alienated and insulted almost everyone who's ever meant anything to you?

**GENET**

Oh so that's it? You came here out of pity? Well I don't need it. The insults I flung were aimed with precision and having landed I can't take them back. I won't. Sartre's a fraud, an intellectual poseur—

**MARIANNE/DE BEAUVOIR**

He's a great man and your friend.

**GENET**

Don't you mean God? After all, it was he who took it upon himself to anoint me a saint. I'm sorry, my dear, I never felt as comfortable as you standing in the "great man's" shadow.

**MARIANNE/DE BEAUVOIR**

Writing Saint Genet was an act of homage.

**GENET**

More like defamation of character. The hubris of the man thinking he could unravel my psyche like an onion.

**MARIANNE/DE BEAUVOIR**

He's waiting for you at the Café de Flore.

**GENET**

He can wait for eternity as far as I'm concerned.

**MARIANNE/DE BEAUVOIR**

Yes, he can. *(beat)* Ingrate!

**GENET**

Succubus!

**MARIANNE/DE BEAUVOIR**

You would have been nothing without Sartre's help.

**GENET**

Cow!

**MARIANNE/DE BEAUVOIR**

Bitch!

**GENET**

Dyke!

**MARIANNE/DE BEAUVOIR**

Darling! I've missed you.

**GENET**

It's my impish charm.

**MARIANNE/DE BEAUVOIR**

Imp, fairy, whatever. (*She steps back up onto the windowsill.*)
Speaking of fairies, Cocteau is also joining us at the Café de Flore.

**GENET**

But my manuscript…

**MARIANNE/DE BEAUVOIR**

What? Oh Jean, you didn't tear it up? Not again. Who knows how
many masterpieces you've destroyed because of your self-indulgent
bouts of depression.

**GENET**

Cocteau?

**MARIANNE/DE BEAUVOIR**

Those veiny hands of his give me the creeps.

**GENET**

You can't stand him.

**MARIANNE/DE BEAUVOIR**

I'm willing to put up with that peacock for your sake, darling.

Maria Vacratsis and William Webster
*photo by David Hawe*

**GENET**

Hold on – if I'm not mistaken hasn't…. Jean has been dead for….
And Sartre – Yes, what am I thinking? They've both been dead for
years. Simone, what are you trying to pull?

**MARIANNE/DE BEAUVOIR**

I've just come to invite you for a few drinks with some old friends.

**GENET**

If you'd kept in touch you'd know that I can't drink anymore.
My kidneys are shot.

**MARIANNE/DE BEAUVOIR**

Oh, darling, I'm sure one little drink won't kill you.

**GENET**

Get out.

**MARIANNE/DE BEAUVOIR**

Really, darling, there's no need to be rude.

**GENET**

Out. NOW!

**MARIANNE/DE BEAUVOIR**

I'll tell Sartre you'll take a rain check.

> *There is a loud gust of wind and MARIANNE/DE BEAUVOIR
> disappears into the night. GENET leans out the window and
> yells out to her.*

**GENET**

You can tell Sartre that he can kiss my ass! *(There is a knocking on the
door.)* Get lost, you barren hag! *(knocking)* Harridan! *(knocking)*
Intellectual leach!

**MARIANNE**

*(offstage)* Monsieur, it's me, Madame Dargenet, is everything all right?
I came to ask you about Pierre…. Monsieur? *(beat)* Monsieur?

> *She enters with a shawl wrapped around her shoulders and sees
> GENET slumping in the windowsill talking in his sleep.*

Oh, Monsieur, you shouldn't be sitting in front of that open window
if you're not well. / The temperature's dropped. It's chilly out there.

> *She moves to close it.*

**GENET**
/ Mmm?

**MARIANNE**
Wake up, Monsieur, you're going to catch a chill napping here.

**GENET**
Oh… it's you…

**MARIANNE**
Sounded like you were having a bad dream so I let myself in.

> *She tactfully manoeuvres GENET from his seat on the windowsill and closes the window. She notices the newspaper.*

Did you read the sad news in the paper?

**GENET**
Mmm?

**MARIANNE**
Simone de Beauvoir passed away yesterday.

**GENET**
Oh yes, I read all about it.

**MARIANNE**
There's talk of a state funeral.

**GENET**
I'm sure the old girl will love it. I think I'll smoke a cigarette to celebrate her passing. *(He retrieves a hidden pack of cigarettes.)*

**MARIANNE**
Oh, Monsieur, do you think that's wise?

**GENET**
*(He lights one up.)* Oh it can't do me much more harm than it already has. And as for Simone, she's always loved smoking, so with any luck she'll end up in a cozy corner of hell. *Bon voyage, de Beauvoir. (He draws on the cigarette and lets out a long puff of smoke.)*

**MARIANNE**
Oh, Monsieur, what a thing to say.

**GENET**
I know, Madame; even I am shocked by the wickedness of me sometimes.

**MARIANNE**

So what did you find out? Anything?

**GENET**

Pierre claims to have had nothing to do with it.

**MARIANNE**

He left here immediately after you spoke to him. Where did he go?

**GENET**

To talk to Luc.

**MARIANNE**

What if he doesn't come back?

**GENET**

Pierre knows if he and Luc try to run they won't get very far before the cops catch up with them.

**MARIANNE**

So it was Luc.

**GENET**

That's what I'm waiting to find out.

**MARIANNE**

I swear, if Pierre had anything to do with this I'll kill him.

**GENET**

There's no need to assume the role of judge, jury and executioner just yet, there's still time.

**MARIANNE**

He will come back won't he?

**GENET**

He'll be back by morning, have no fear.

**MARIANNE**

I won't sleep a wink tonight. *(She turns to leave.)*

**GENET**

Oh Madame, before you go, may I ask you something?

**MARIANNE**

What is it?

**GENET**

Who does Pierre take after most – you or Gaston?

**MARIANNE**

Well, I... well I think he takes after... well, to be honest with you...
I don't think he takes after either of us very much. He's actually more
like my younger sister Camille. She was more of a rebel when we were
kids than I was.

**GENET**

Just like Pierre.

**MARIANNE**

Why do you ask me that, Monsieur?

**GENET**

Oh, just curious. Now you try and get some sleep and don't worry.
Everything is going to be fine.

**MARIANNE**

I hope so. Goodnight, Monsieur.

> *She exits. GENET reaches into his mouth and takes out the
> unswallowed pill and disposes of it. He picks up the leopard
> notebook and crosses over to the window, sits and begins to write.*
>
> *Blackout.*

### SCENE FOUR

> *Lights come up on PIERRE standing beside GENET who is at
> the window. PIERRE has a backpack containing the stolen goods.*

**PIERRE**

*(loud whisper)* Jean... Jean wake up. Jean?

**GENET**

*(His eyes snap open.)* You're late.

**PIERRE**

Oh jeez, don't do that. You nearly gave me a heart attack. I was
knocking at the door and you didn't answer, and I thought...

> *GENET crosses to the desk and puts the notebook on it.*

**GENET**

You better have what I asked for because you're late and that means
the hunt is on. And only I can call it off.

**PIERRE**

Yeah – no – I have it, I have it right here.

*PIERRE takes the manuscript out of the backpack and gives it to GENET.*

**GENET**

Not a moment too soon…

**PIERRE**

So there it is, every page.

**GENET**

Yes, yes it's you, it's you.

**PIERRE**

This is yours, too.

*PIERRE hands him his wallet.*

**GENET**

Oh— *(He looks into his wallet and sees the money is still there.)* My wallet, and not a franc missing. You're too kind.

**PIERRE**

Yeah right, whatever. Uh, so then everything's cool?

**GENET**

Yes, yes everything's… "cool."

**PIERRE**

Great, so that means you'll call off your goons?

**GENET**

What's that?

**PIERRE**

Those goons you've got out there looking for me and Luc. You're going to call them off aren't you?

**GENET**

Oh yes, well I wouldn't worry about that.

**PIERRE**

You said you'd have us killed!

**GENET**

I lied.

**PIERRE**

You lied? You prick – you lying – You have no idea what I went through to get that manuscript back to you.

**GENET**

Yes, well it was terribly inconvenient for both of us, wasn't it? So stop your whining and consider yourself lucky.

**PIERRE**

(chuckles) Yeah I'm real lucky…. You tricked me…. Huh, that's hilarious.

**GENET**

I'm glad you find it amusing.

> PIERRE continues to chuckle to himself.

**PIERRE**

Yeah, twice in one night, you've got to laugh.

**GENET**

Mmmm?

**PIERRE**

I was expecting Luc to freak out when I told him what would happen to us if we didn't give your manuscript back.

**GENET**

Did he?

**PIERRE**

No, he cracked up and called you a "nasty hard-core old bugger." Then he gave me the manuscript, no problem.

**GENET**

So then what took you so long?

**PIERRE**

Well… after he gave it back he offered me a beer and we smoked a joint, and then one thing led to another…

**GENET**

As these things do.

**PIERRE**

I still thought he was going to Greece and… I had decided that I… I wanted to… give myself to him completely… before I told him I was going to go with him…

**GENET**

And in the height of passion when Luc finally impaled you with lust you... opened the locket of your heart and exposed the naked bloom within?

**PIERRE**

Yeah... I told him... I told him that I loved him...

**GENET**

Then when ambrosia had shot through the universe of your soul he pulled out and...?

**PIERRE**

He started yelling, freaking out...

**GENET**

Tearing apart the petals of the rose...

**PIERRE**

Everything is so fucked up! Why are people so fucked up?

**GENET**

Oh, I don't know; greed, envy, betrayal, money, lack of sex, lack of sleep? Take your pick.

*The lights snap to Mettray as LUC/VILLEROY enters.*
*PIERRE assumes the role of YOUNG GENET.*

**LUC/VILLEROY**

Jean – Jean, have you heard? I'd almost forgotten it was ever going to happen!

**PIERRE/YOUNG GENET**

What is it, Villeroy? What are you so excited about?

**LUC/VILLEROY**

I'm getting out.

**PIERRE/YOUNG GENET**

Out?

**LUC/VILLEROY**

Yeah, I got the news this morning. Hell, I just about fell down when Lardet told me. I've been in here so long I could hardly believe it. I don't know what I'm going to do first when I get out of here. I'm free!

**PIERRE/YOUNG GENET**

When do you leave?

**LUC/VILLEROY**

Tomorrow.

>    *PIERRE/YOUNG GENET begins to cry.*

Now don't start crying. Hey, come on now, none of that. Don't want the other mugs seeing you cry, do you?

**PIERRE/YOUNG GENET**

I don't care.

**LUC/VILLEROY**

Come on, pull yourself together. You should be happy for me. I'm getting out of this God-forsaken place.

**PIERRE/YOUNG GENET**

I know, but what'll happen to me when you're gone?

**LUC/VILLEROY**

You don't have to worry, it's all taken care of.

**PIERRE/YOUNG GENET**

What do you mean?

**LUC/VILLEROY**

I'm going to need some money when I get out of here, so I sold you to another guy. He'll take care of you if you just do like he says.

**PIERRE/YOUNG GENET**

I won't.

**LUC/VILLEROY**

You trying to make me look like a fool?

**PIERRE/YOUNG GENET**

No, I—

**LUC/VILLEROY**

Then don't start acting like some stupid jilted bride.

**PIERRE/YOUNG GENET**

You expect me to play the part of the highborn lady who's left behind to suffer in silence? Fuck you!

**LUC/VILLEROY**

We all have our parts to play, Jean, it doesn't mean anything.

**PIERRE/YOUNG GENET**

/ It means I love you.

**GENET**

/ It means I love you.

**LUC/VILLEROY**

Love? We were just screwing around for Christ's sake! I'm not a faggot. You're the one who likes taking it up the ass, not me! What do you expect me to do now? *(laughs)* Say I love you too? You're not serious—

**PIERRE/YOUNG GENET**

Don't laugh at me—

**LUC/VILLEROY**

So what, now I'm supposed to pity you? Fuck you!

*LUC/VILLEROY exits. The lighting returns to the present.*

**PIERRE**

He kept yelling, "I'm not a faggot, you're the one who likes it up the ass." Are you listening?

*GENET looks for the leopard notebook.*

**GENET**

Yes... yes, sounds like he screwed you all right.

**PIERRE**

Then he told me that he had made up with his parents, and he was going off to Africa to meet them on vacation. That's when I lost it.

*GENET finds the notebook.*

**GENET**

Who threw the first punch?

**PIERRE**

I did.

**GENET**

*(starts writing)* Good for you.

**PIERRE**

Then he took a few swings at me and told me to fuck off and die.

**GENET**

Crude, but effective.

**PIERRE**

But why couldn't he—?

**GENET**

Love you? *(He looks up from the notebook.)* Because when his "big cock" is engorged with blood, there's not enough left to fill his heart.

**PIERRE**

Was it all me? Didn't he feel anything?

**GENET**

Of course. Lust and then fear by the sound of it.

**PIERRE**

Fear?

**GENET**

Oh come on, don't be such a dunce. After finally surrendering completely you spoke the forbidden word, "love." Oops, he wasn't expecting that. And then, like a lot of men who are taken by surprise by that word; his dick shrank to the size of an acorn, setting off a gag reflex that released the vomit of disgust he puked in your face.

**PIERRE**

But he liked it, why would it disgust him?

**GENET**

Because acts of pleasure veiled in denial produce barbs of self-loathing that transmogrify the insecure into tyrants, and free men into slaves.

**PIERRE**

I'm not a slave.

**GENET**

No? Then you have a plan? Because you have to have a plan if you're going to overthrow a tyrant.

**PIERRE**

Luc might be an asshole but he's not a tyrant.

**GENET**

No? He got you to steal, betray your family, give up your virginity, and then he treated you like shit. And if he walked in that door right now and told you he loved you, you'd run into his waiting arms and forgive him instantly.

**PIERRE**

No—

**GENET**

Liar. I told you the other day that tyrants come in many guises. But most of us fail to recognize them before it's to late because we're blinded by this ineffable emotion called "Love." Be it love of country, ideology, religion, filial or the idiotic puffery that passes for romance these days. They're all yokes when somebody else is pulling the reins.

**PIERRE**

Okay, so Luc's a tyrant and I'm a slave. So what am I supposed to do?

**GENET**

*(stops writing)* How about letting me get some sleep? You got yourself into this and now you have the gall to ask me for advice? I'm not your fucking grandfather for Christ's sake! You wanted to play with the big boys, so you figure it out and stop sniffing up my ass for sympathy. What are you waiting for? Get the hell out! I'm a sick man and I've wasted enough time on you as it is. *(He crosses to the door.)*

**PIERRE**

Wait. I have a plan. *(GENET stops,)* Luc's dad has a camcorder video camera. Last summer his parents went away for a couple of days so I stayed over at Luc's.

**GENET**

Ah, and you explored the world of home video?

**PIERRE**

We were so blasted I don't even remember whose idea it was.

*GENET moves toward the door.*

**GENET**

Tich-tich-tich.

**PIERRE**

It's true, I don't. Next morning he forgot to take it out of the camcorder. So, I grabbed it and kept it.

*GENET picks up the notebook and starts writing.*

**GENET**

So what's it going to be? Blackmail?

**PIERRE**

No.

**GENET**

Aw.

**PIERRE**

I'm going to mail it to his parents free of charge.

**GENET**

A crystalline annihilation.

**PIERRE**

When they get back they're going to find a little package waiting for them. And when they open it up and see what's on that video, they'll shit their pants and hit the roof at the same time.

> *GENET continues to write and chuckles to himself. The sound of footsteps approaching down the hallway is heard.*

What are you writing?

> *There is a loud knocking on the door. We hear GASTON's voice offstage.*

**GASTON**

*(offstage)* Monsieur! *(GENET puts the notebook down.)* Monsieur, we need to talk—

**MARIANNE**

*(offstage, loud whisper)* Gaston, lower your voice or you'll wake up the whole floor.

> *PIERRE and GENET listen.*

**GASTON**

*(offstage)* I don't care. I want to know what the hell's been going on here! *(Knocks on the door.)* Monsieur wake up, we need to talk.

> *GENET gestures toward the armoire as PIERRE grabs the duffle bag. GENET crosses to the door as PIERRE steps inside the armoire.*

**GENET**

Yes? What is it?

**MARIANNE**

*(offstage)* Monsieur, I'm sorry but I couldn't sleep—

**GASTON**

(*offstage*) She told me what you two have been up to so you better open this door—

*GENET opens the door. GASTON and MARIANNE enter.*

**MARIANNE**

Oh, Monsieur, I was just too worried I couldn't keep it to myself anymore.

**GASTON**

Did he tell you where this Luc kid is staying?

**GENET**

No.

**GASTON**

And you really think that little punk's going to give the stuff back?

**GENET**

We're not even sure if he has it yet.

**GASTON**

Oh come on, you wouldn't have sent Pierre over there if you didn't think he had it! I don't know who you think you are, Monsieur, messing around in our family business.

**GENET**

It became my business when my manuscript was stolen.

**GASTON**

Soon it's going to be police business.

**GENET**

I was just trying to give your son the opportunity of avoiding being arrested. I've never been a father myself, but I'm sure I wouldn't want to see a son of mine go to prison.

**GASTON**

Yes, well he's not your son, is he?

**GENET**

No, and he's not yours either.

**GASTON**

/ Hey—

**MARIANNE**

/ What?

**GENET**

Hypocrite! Coming in here telling me to mind my own business. When you were in here the other afternoon spilling the beans about her sister Camille, dumping Pierre on your doorstep. Like I give a shit hearing him complain about the bastard he's had to raise.

**GASTON**

I never said he was Camille's kid.

**MARIANNE**

Why would you even mention it?

**GASTON**

I – ah…

**GENET**

I felt sorry for the kid…. His mother having to give him up because of well… you know.

**MARIANNE**

Have you been going around telling people about Camille?

**GASTON**

No, I never said anything about Camille—

**GENET**

And I suppose you didn't say you wanted to boot Pierre out? Well I guess getting him arrested is the next best thing.

**GASTON**

You shut up! You've caused enough trouble around here!

**MARIANNE**

Don't talk to one of our guests like that! At least he's shown some concern for Pierre's welfare.

**GASTON**

He's trying to help the kid get away with a crime.

**MARIANNE**

And you'd rather see Pierre get arrested?

**GASTON**

Yes, damn it! If that's what it takes to give that kid a kick in the ass! Don't look at me like that.

**MARIANNE**

Maybe if you would have shown him a little – It was stupid of me to think that after all these years you would have finally… never mind. I'm sorry, Monsieur, I should never have gotten you involved in this, despite your good intentions—

**GASTON**

Why are you apologizing? He's the one who's been interfering—

**MARIANNE**

Gaston will you just shut up! Haven't you said enough? Airing our family's dirty laundry in front of a perfect stranger?

**GASTON**

I didn't – he – all I said was – Look, we wouldn't be arguing about this if we'd just told Pierre the truth – his aunt Camille is really his mother and she couldn't be bothered to raise him herself because she's still out there running wild!

**MARIANNE**

That's enough, Gaston, enough! *(She stares him down.)* I told you when we took him in if you didn't like the arrangement you didn't have to stay…. That option is still open to you. *(Beat. GASTON abruptly leaves.)*

**GENET**

You really love that kid.

**MARIANNE**

From the moment I laid eyes on him.

**GENET**

Yes, Madame, I'm sure your heart has always been in the right place.

**MARIANNE**

Well I should go and deal with Gaston…. If he's still here. Once again I apologize…. Please don't think badly of us.

**GENET**

Don't be ridiculous, every family has a skeleton or two hanging in their closet.

**MARIANNE**

I'll check with you in the morning.

**GENET**

Yes, and if he isn't back by then we'll call the cops.

**MARIANNE**

Goodnight, Monsieur.

*She turns to exit and as she crosses to the door she notices the manuscript on the desk. She stops and then walks over to it and picks it up. She looks at GENET questioningly. Beat. He nods and looks toward the armoire. Beat. MARIANNE speaks toward the armoire.*

And, Monsieur, if you do see Pierre, you be sure to tell him that his mama will always be here for him no matter what.

**GENET**

I'll make sure he gets that information.

**MARIANNE**

Thank you.

*She puts the manuscript down and exits. Beat.*

**GENET**

Okay, the coast is clear you can come out now. Pierre?

*There is no response. GENET takes a step toward the armoire as the door begins to open. A bright light shines into the room. GASTON/LARDET appears in the armoire.*

**GASTON/LARDET**

Welcome to Mettray, number 192.102. I am the director of the colony, Monsieur Lardet.

**GENET**

So it's you they've sent for me this time, is it?

*We hear the voice-overs of the boys of Mettray.*

**BOYS OF METTRAY**

*(voice-over)* My God, I thank you for letting me live through another day.

**GENET**

I'm not ready—

**GASTON/LARDET**

Very few ever are, but sentence has been passed.

**BOYS OF METTRAY**

*(voice-over)* Please give me the blessing of sleeping well tonight.

*GENET rushes to the armoire.*

**GENET**

Not yet! My mother was Joan of Arc, Marie Antoinette, Madame Curie! My father was the King of Brooms! I sprang from the belly of the earth. The children fucked, massacred, and burned by Gilles de Rais nourished my roots. I am the orphan bastard of Apollo whose seed spawned the kings of France.

**BOYS OF METTRAY**

*(voice-over)* May you take pity on us.

**GASTON/LARDET**

And when did you get crowned King of the Shit-pile?

**GENET**

When I started turning the shit I swallowed into gold.

*He slams the armoire doors shut. The lighting state returns to the present. We hear PIERRE's voice coming from inside the armoire.*

**PIERRE**

Hey what's going on? Let me out of here!

**GENET**

I told you, I'm not ready.

**PIERRE**

I don't give a shit if you're ready or not, let me out of here! *(He forces his way out of the armoire.)*

What the fuck were you doing?

*GENET crosses to the desk.*

**GENET**

I thought you were…. I thought…

**PIERRE**

You thought what? That you'd drop that bomb about me not being their kid and then keep me locked up in that thing and torment me?

*GENET picks up the leopard notebook and begins writing. He writes as he winces in pain.*

**GENET**

To have been dangerous for a thousandth of a second, to have been handsome for a thousandth of a thousandth of a second, to have felt love for just a single heartbeat – these are the delights in which we taste paradise for a moment—

**PIERRE**

I don't give a shit about all that!

**GENET**

And every moment after that is filled with the desire to taste it again.

**PIERRE**

What the hell are you writing?

> *He grabs the notebooks from GENET's hands. He reads to himself for a moment and flips through the pages.*

**GENET**

Give it back! It means nothing to you!

**PIERRE**

Oh, it means nothing to me? *(He reads from the notebook.)* "The trap was set and it was just a matter of time before the young fool took the bait"? *(He flips to another page.)* "The foster father obviously resented the years spent raising the child of a whore"?! "He sees the thug he loves encased in armour made of gold… but soon he'll realize it was brass all along"?! You've been using me!

**GENET**

Every writer needs inspiration.

**PIERRE**

But your manuscript, what if we kept it?

**GENET**

It's all in Gallimard's hands.

**PIERRE**

Your publisher has a copy?

**GENET**

Only a fool doesn't make a copy.

**PIERRE**

You never gave a shit about it.

**GENET**

Untrue, because without it...

**PIERRE**

You wouldn't have gotten your new story.

**GENET**

Exactly. Now if you don't mind.

> GENET *reaches for the notebook but* PIERRE *holds it out of reach.*

**PIERRE**

I do mind – you – you never gave a shit about what could have happened to me—

**GENET**

Why should I? Who are you to me? You played your hand and I played mine. We made our choices, good or bad, and now we have to live with them.

**PIERRE**

That's all you've ever done, isn't it? Used people. Maybe that's why you're here alone—

> GENET *reaches for the notebook and* PIERRE *dodges him.*

**GENET**

Oh please, let's not get maudlin.

**PIERRE**

Alone... except for your words.

> PIERRE *holds the notebook and prepares to rip it apart.*

**GENET**

Don't—

**PIERRE**

You asked me if people still read? Yeah, they read but I'll bet they haven't been reading anything of yours for awhile – huh? Have they?

**GENET**

So it's been you all along?

**PIERRE**

What the fuck are you talking about now?

**GENET**

I won't let you take me down, boy.

**PIERRE**

You know what you are without your words? Just a sick lonely old man— *(rips a page)*

**GENET**

No!

**PIERRE**

Just like the rest of the fossils that have been forgotten on this floor. *(rips a page)*

**GENET**

No!

**PIERRE**

Just like a thousand other forgotten "writers" that nobody gives a shit about anymore.

> *GENET rushes at PIERRE and grabs for the notebook, but PIERRE is too fast and tears the notebook apart.*

**GENET**

No!

> *PIERRE continues to tear apart the notebook until it is in shreds.*

**PIERRE**

Don't worry, Jean, you can always re-write it from memory. Yeah, we'll always have these memories.

**GENET**

Fuck off.

> *PIERRE exits. GENET sits alone for a moment and is gripped by another spasm of pain. The armoire door begins to open. A bright light shines into the room from the inside of the armoire as GENET is transported to Mettray. GASTON/LARDET appears in the doorway of the armoire.*

**GASTON/LARDET**

Welcome to Mettray, number 192.102. I am the director of the colony, Monsieur Lardet.

> *GENET begins to search for his pills.*

**GENET**

Yes – yes I know who you are.

**BOYS OF METTRAY**

(voice-over) My God, I thank you for letting me live through another day.

**·GASTON/LARDET**

Despite what you might have heard, number 192.102, the colony of Mettray is not a prison for boys. We are an agricultural commune of "supervised freedom."

*He finds his pills and desperately tries to open the bottle.*

**BOYS OF METTRAY**

(voice-over) Please give me the blessing of sleeping well tonight.

**GASTON/LARDET**

In this place the ideals of Rousseau prevail. There are no walls or fences, only laurel bushes and flowerbeds. Fresh air and plenty of sunlight nourish the soil and purify the soul.

**GENET**

Yes, I remember those goddamn flowers, they terrified me!

*He opens the bottle and the pills spill on the floor.*

Shit—

*As he gets down on his knees to collect the pills, he's gripped by a heart attack.*

**BOYS OF METTRAY**

(voice-over) Please grant us the blessings to be worthy of your love. And please let it be over, let it be over, let it be over!

*GENET collapses. As the light begins to fade the images of huge colourful flowers cover the walls.*

**GASTON/LARDET**

Silence! Sleep!

*Blackout.*

*The End.*

Ed has been a constant member of the Canadian theatre community for years, doing everything from directing, writing, dramaturgy, acting, teaching, to producing. He has been the recipient of numerous awards for his theatrical adventures, including the Pauline McGibbon Award for directing, the Chalmers Playwriting Award for *A Secret Life* and two Dora Awards for Outstanding Production for the plays *The Other Side of the Closet* and *White Trash Blue Eyes*. As an actor, Ed was also nominated for a Dora for his performance in *Video Cabaret's The Life and Times of Mackenzie King*, and is the proud recipient of a Harold Alternative Theatre Award.